OCEAN OF DHARMA

OCEAN OF DHARMA

The Everyday Wisdom of Chögyam Trungpa

Compiled and Edited by
Carolyn Rose Gimian

Shambhala
Boston & London · 2008

Shambhala Publications, Inc.
Horticultural Hall
300 Massachusetts Avenue
Boston, Massachusetts 02115
www.shambhala.com

9 8 7 6 5 4 3 2 1
FIRST EDITION

Printed in the United States of America

♾ This edition is printed on acid-free paper that meets the American National Standards Institute z39.48 Standard.

Distributed in the United States by Random House, Inc., and in Canada by Random House of Canada Ltd

Library of Congress Cataloging-in-Publication Data
Trungpa, Chögyam, 1939–1987.
Ocean of dharma: the everyday wisdom of Chögyam Trungpa / Chögyam Trungpa; edited by Carolyn Rose Gimian.
p. cm.
Includes bibliographical references.
ISBN 978-1-59030-536-2 (pbk.: alk. paper)
1. Buddhist meditations. I. Gimian, Carolyn Rose. II. Title.
BQ5572.T78 2008
294.3'4432—dc22
2007033814

CONTENTS

EDITOR'S PREFACE

This book contains 365 quotations from the teachings of Chögyam Trungpa Rinpoche, one of the most influential Buddhist teachers of our time. *Ocean of Dharma* is the literal translation of "Chögyam," and it aptly describes the profound and vast nature of the teachings he offered during the more than twenty years he spent teaching in the West. ("Rinpoche" is a title for realized teachers in the Tibetan tradition, which means "Precious One" or "Precious Jewel.")

There are many ways to read this book: You can open it to any page and see what you find. You can read a quote every morning or every night, or before or after your daily practice of meditation (or other contemplative disciplines). These quotes may stimulate your intellect and intuition, logical thought and feelings. They may confound. They may provide moments of "Aha!" How you engage this material is personal, and each reader's experience will be different. These quotations not only present ultimate wisdom but relative, immediate truth, the means to realize this wisdom, and advice on how to apply your understanding in everyday life.

Chögyam Trungpa wrote that wisdom can only be taught in the form of a hint. Because of your own inherent wisdom, having received that hint, you can pick up the message spontaneously. *Ocean of Dharma* presents you with many hints about how to be and how to see: how to be a warrior without anger in this world, living with both tenderness and bravery; how to wake up and experience the brilliance and majesty of life; and how to share that with others. All of this is based on the courage to be realistic and genuine, and there are many quotes here that encourage the fearless acceptance of life as it is.

There are a number of approaches to contemplating what you read. You may deliberately reflect on a quote, probing it, looking at it from every angle. Or you may savor it, like slowly dissolving a piece of chocolate in your mouth, tasting every nuance of its sweet and bitter flavor. Or you may read a quote and then forget about it, not trying to do anything deliberate with it at all. Later, it may arise spontaneously in your mind. Sometimes wisdom hits you full in the face, like turning on the light in a dark room and being shocked by what you encounter. Sometimes it works its way into your heart and mind, only emerging after a long period of gestation.

Chögyam Trungpa described wisdom as a mirror, one which helps you to join heaven and earth. In this analogy, heaven is electricity or daylight; earth is your uncombed hair, your face, your unshaven beard. The mirror allows you to bring the two together so that you can see yourself, comb your hair, wash your face, and shave. In that sense, wisdom is both illuminating and practical—it lets you perceive yourself and your world and it provides a means to do something about what you see.

On the one hand, wisdom knows no master. It does not belong to anyone. On the other hand, its unique articulation is often what allows us to recognize it. *Ocean of Dharma* presents wisdom as viewed and expressed by a grand master of Buddhism in America. Twenty years after his death, he is still one of the best-selling Buddhist authors in the West. Why so? Because his teachings are so penetrating and so applicable to contemporary experience, yet they are also timeless. All of those qualities are manifest in these short quotations, as much as in the whole works from which they are drawn. There is something so unusual, uncanny, and personal about this man, and by reading his work, one is entering into a relationship with him, in a sense. I would be amazed if you could read this book from beginning to end without being deeply affected.

Many quotes deal with experiences that are inspired by or arise from the practice of sitting meditation. Yet it is not necessary to be a meditator in order to appreciate and benefit from this book. In one of the selections, Chögyam Trungpa says that anyone who creates a work of art meditates, whether they call the activity meditation or not. Wherever one finds a gap or a sense of space in life, whatever it is that one does that provides a feeling of ground, earth, or being—fundamentally, that is meditation. With that in mind, anyone could connect with the material in this book.

For those curious about meditation but untutored in the technique, an introduction to the practice of meditation appears in the back matter, adapted from *Shambhala: The Sacred Path of the Warrior.* Anyone who wants to practice meditation would be well-advised to get personal instruction. Purely learning to meditate from a book is like learning to cook from a cookbook without ever having been in the kitchen before.

This book evolved from an e-mail service I developed called Ocean of Dharma Quotes of the Week.* (To subscribe, go to www.oceanofdharma.com.) While most of the quotations in this collection are from published sources (both well-known and obscure), some material appears in print here for the first time. My sources include unpublished transcripts, sourcebooks that are not in wide distribution, as well as classic, best-selling works. The source of each quotation is identified at the end of the book.

Many times while I was working on this manuscript, I found that the quotations and my life intersected in unexpected ways. For example, one afternoon I was having an argument with my husband. We parted in a huff and I went back to working on the book. To my surprise, the next quote I read was one on marriage and regarding communication with your partner as sacred. Many people who subscribe to Ocean of Dharma have reported similar experiences. The quote arrives in the e-mail just when they are working with the particular issue it addresses. This unplanned but often

* I began the Ocean of Dharma e-mails on April 9, 2003. A week after I "spontaneously" started this Listserv, an old friend of mine wrote to tell me that Trungpa Rinpoche had posted his *only* message to the Internet on April 9, 1983, exactly twenty years earlier to the day. (Few people had access to the Internet then, but Rinpoche did through a group of his students who were working on developing it.) It seemed to be a very auspicious coincidence.

reported synchronicity is one of the reasons that I came to believe that a book based on the quotes would be helpful.

I have reworked, reordered, and retitled a great deal of material. I edited the selections from unedited and unpublished talks and seminars, and in a few instances I have reedited passages from published sources, almost always those originally edited by myself. Questions and answers have been edited into expository statements. I have also condensed quotations, inserted definitions of Buddhist terms, and in a few places I have made gender or voice changes or added a phrase for clarification. All of this has been done in the interest of making this material as immediate and accessible as possible in this context.

Like an ocean, like a hint, like a mirror, wisdom is vast, ineffable, and luminous. So too is the mind of the wisdom holder Chögyam Trungpa Rinpoche. Rinpoche liked to tell stories about Padmasambhava, the father of Buddhism in Tibet. According to tradition, Padmasambhava wrote down a number of teachings and buried them in the mountains of Tibet so that they would be discovered by future generations. Reflecting on this practice, Trungpa Rinpoche wrote:

> Padmasambhava developed an approach for communicating with future generations. He thought, "If I leave an example of my teaching behind, even if people of future generations do not experience my example, just hearing or reading my words alone could cause a spiritual atomic bomb to explode in a future time."

May this book serve that purpose. May it be a delightful firework exploding in the darkness of our confusion, reminding us that this darkness is also a great inviting space, in which confusion is also wisdom.

Carolyn Rose Gimian
Halifax, Nova Scotia

EDITOR'S ACKNOWLEDGMENTS

SUBSCRIBERS TO the Ocean of Dharma Quotes of the Week Listserv sent in their suggestions for quotes to be included in this book. I would like to thank everyone for their suggestions, whether or not they are included in the current volume. I would also like to thank subscribers for their general feedback on the quotes and their endless encouragement over the last five years.

Material in *Ocean of Dharma* is taken from more than two dozen books and another dozen published sources, as well as many unpublished sources. I would like to thank a small army of people who, from 1967 on, have recorded, transcribed, archived, digitized, edited, and published the material from which I drew. In particular, I would like to thank the editors of Chögyam Trungpa's books.

I would like to thank the Shambhala Archives for preserving the tapes, transcripts, and other records of Chögyam Trungpa's life and teachings and for giving me extensive access to material; Vajradhatu Publications, and their staff (including the staff at the *Dot*) for permission to quote from their publications and for advertising the Listserv; the *Shambhala Sun* and *Elephant*—and many individuals on their staffs—for use of material published in these magazines and for help advertising the Listserv; Barbara Gates for the idea for an article in *Inquiring Mind* using quotes by Chögyam Trungpa on a sense of humor, several of which made their way into this book; Fabrice Midal, who compiled a book of quotations by Chögyam Trungpa that was published in France, for encouragement and feedback; Lenny Jacobs, Liz Shaw, and other folks at Shambhala Publications for technical support for the Ocean of Dharma e-mail service, the Chögyam Trungpa and Ocean of Dharma web pages, and overall interest in the Ocean of Dharma list; Peter Turner, the president of Shambhala Publications, and Eden Steinberg, my editor there, for help shaping the idea of this book; and Jim Zaccaria and Daniel Urban for design. Special thanks to Eden for her careful reading of the early drafts of the book. Her comments and suggestions greatly improved the manuscript. And my thanks to Jim and Jenny for their appreciation, love, and support.

Finally, I would like to thank Diana J. Mukpo, Sakyong Mipham Rinpoche, and the other members of the Mukpo family for their ongoing support for the publication of the work of Chögyam Trungpa, and the author himself for giving us these teachings and for the privilege of working with a few drops from this water of life.

OCEAN OF DHARMA

I

The Challenge of Warriorship

THE CHALLENGE OF WARRIORSHIP is to live fully in the world as it is and to find within this world, with all its paradoxes, the essence of nowness. If we open our eyes, if we open our minds, if we open our hearts, we will find that this world is a magical place. It is not magical because it tricks us or changes unexpectedly into something else, but it is magical because it can *be* so vividly, so brilliantly. However, the discovery of that magic can happen only when we transcend our embarrassment about being alive, when we have the bravery to proclaim the goodness and dignity of human life, without either hesitation or arrogance.

2

A Good Journey

OUR LIFE is an endless journey. It is like a broad highway that extends infinitely into the distance. The practice of meditation provides a vehicle to travel on that road. Our journey consists of constant ups and downs, hope and fear, but it is a good journey. The practice of meditation allows us to experience all the textures of the roadway, which is what the journey is all about. Through the practice of meditation, we begin to find that within ourselves there is no fundamental complaint about anything or anyone at all.

3

Unlearning

MEDITATION IS THE ONLY way to relate with neurosis and self-deception. In this case, meditation does not mean concentrating on objects or trying to intensify certain psychic faculties or anything of that nature. It is simply creating a space, a space in which we can unlearn and undo our subconscious gossip, our hidden fears and hidden hopes, and begin to bring them out. Meditation is simply providing space through the discipline of sitting down and doing nothing. Doing nothing is extremely difficult. At the beginning we can only try to do nothing by imitating doing nothing. And then hopefully we can develop gradually from there.

4

What Is a Warrior?

Anyone who is interested in hearing the dharma, anyone who is interested in finding out about oneself, and anyone who is interested in practicing meditation is basically a warrior. The approach of cowardice is looking for some tremendous external help, whether it comes from the sky or from the earth. You are afraid of actually seeing yourself; therefore you use spirituality or religion as a seeming way of seeing yourself without looking directly at yourself at all. Basically, when people are embarrassed about themselves, there's no fearlessness involved. Therefore, anybody who is interested in looking at oneself, finding out about oneself, and practicing on the spot could be regarded as a warrior.

5

Facing Ourselves

We have a fear of facing ourselves. That is the obstacle. Experiencing the innermost core of our existence is very embarrassing to a lot of people. A lot of people turn to something that they hope will liberate them without their having to face themselves. That is impossible. We can't do that. We have to be honest with ourselves. We have to see our gut, our excrement, our most undesirable parts. We have to see them. That is the foundation of warriorship, basically speaking. Whatever is there, we have to face it, we have to look at it, study it, work with it, and practice meditation with it.

6

Our Human Endowment

People often talk about trying to hold back their tears, but as human beings, we should take pride in our capacity to be sad and happy. We mustn't ignore the preciousness of our human birth or take it for granted. It is extremely precious and very powerful. We cannot ignore our basic human endowment.

7

Creative Revolution

Buddha was a great revolutionary in his way of thinking. He even denied the existence of Brahma, or God, the Creator of the world. He determined to accept nothing which he had not first discovered for himself. This does not mean to say that he disregarded the great and ancient tradition of India. He respected it very much. His was not an anarchistic attitude in any negative sense, nor was it revolutionary in the way the communists are. His was real, positive revolution. He developed the creative side of revolution, which is not trying to get help from anyone else, but finding out for oneself. By developing such a revolutionary attitude one learns a great deal.

8

Seeing for Yourself

WHAT IS IMPORTANT is to get beyond the pattern of mental concepts which we have formed. One must learn to be a skillful scientist and not accept anything at all. Everything must be seen through one's own microscope and one has to reach one's own conclusions in one's own way. Until we do that, there is no savior, no guru, no blessings, and no guidance that could be of any help.

9

The Starting Point

It would be foolish to study more advanced subjects before we are familiar with the starting point, the nature of ego. Speculations about the goal become mere fantasy. These speculations may take the form of advanced ideas and descriptions of spiritual experiences, but they only exploit the weaker aspects of human nature, our expectations and desires to see and hear something colorful, something extraordinary. If we begin our study with these dreams of extraordinary, "enlightening," and dramatic experiences, then we will build up our expectations and preconceptions so that later, when we are actually working on the path, our minds will be occupied largely with what will be rather than with what *is*. It is destructive and not fair to people to play on their weaknesses, their expectations and dreams, rather than to present the realistic starting point of what they are. It is necessary, therefore, to start on what we are and why we are searching.

10

Friendliness to Oneself

THE RECOGNITION of sacredness comes from developing a basic sense of gentleness toward ourselves, so that the irritation of being stuck with oneself is taken away. When that kind of friendliness to oneself has occurred, then one also develops friendliness toward the rest of the world, at the same time. At that point, sadness, loneliness, and wretchedness begin to dissipate. We begin to develop a sense of humor. We don't get so pissed off if we have a bad cup of coffee in the morning. A natural sense of dignity begins to occur.

11

Buddha Is Everywhere

Buddha can't be avoided. Buddha is everywhere. Enlightenment possibilities are all over the place. Whether you're going to get married tomorrow, whether you're going to die tomorrow, whatever you may feel, that familiar awake quality is everywhere, all the time. From this point of view, everything is a footprint of Buddha, anything that goes on, whether we regard it as sublime or ridiculous. Everything we do—breathing, farting, getting mosquito bites, having fantastic ideas about reality, thinking clever thoughts, flushing the toilet—whatever occurs is a footprint.

12

Chaos Is the Inspiration

VERY BEAUTIFUL SITUATIONS have developed using chaos as part of the enlightened approach. There is chaos of all kinds developing all the time: psychological disorder, social disorder, metaphysical disorder, or physical disorder, constantly happening. If you are trying to stop those situations, you are looking for external means of liberating yourself, another answer. But if we are able to look into the basic situation, then chaos is the inspiration, confusion is the inspiration.

13

What Is Fear?

THE ESSENCE OF COWARDICE is not acknowledging the reality of fear. Fear can take many forms. Logically, we know we can't live forever. We are petrified of our death. On another level, we are afraid that we can't handle the demands of the world. This fear expresses itself as a feeling of inadequacy. We feel that our own lives are overwhelming, and confronting the rest of the world is more overwhelming. Then there is abrupt fear, or panic, that arises when new situations occur suddenly in our lives. When we feel that we can't handle them, we jump or twitch. Sometimes fear manifests in the form of restlessness: doodles on a notepad, playing with our fingers, or fidgeting in our chairs. We feel that we have to keep ourselves moving all the time, like an engine running in a motorcar. The pistons go up and down, up and down. As long as the pistons keep moving, we feel safe. Otherwise, we are afraid we might die on the spot.

14

Regal Existence

The discipline of meditation is designed so that everybody can become a good person. Everybody should have a regal existence. When you sit on your meditation cushion, don't hesitate: try to be regal. Synchronize mind and body and try to have good physical posture. In meditation, you should keep everything very simple. Work with everything simply and directly, keep a good posture, follow the breath, and then project your mind. Let your awareness go out with your breath.

15

The Buddha and Basic Goodness

Buddhists try to follow the example of the Buddha. The Buddha was an Indian prince who decided to abandon his palace and his kingdom in order to find out what life is all about. He was looking for the meaning of life, the purpose of life. He wanted to know who and what he was. So he went and practiced meditation, and he ate very little. He meditated for six years, twenty-four hours a day. And at the end of those six years he discovered something: He realized that people don't have to struggle so much. We don't have to give in so much to our hassles, our pain, our discomfort.

The Buddha discovered that there is something in us known as basic goodness. Therefore, we don't have to condemn ourselves for being bad or naughty. The Buddha taught what he had learned to the rest of mankind. What he taught then—twenty-five hundred years ago—is still being taught and practiced. The important point for us is to realize that we are basically good. Our only problem is that sometimes we don't actually acknowledge that goodness. We don't see it, so we blame somebody else or we blame ourselves. That is a mistake. We don't have to blame others, and we don't have to feel nasty or angry. Fundamental goodness is always with us, always in us.

16

The Practice of Meditation

THERE HAVE BEEN a number of misconceptions regarding meditation. Some people regard it as a trancelike state of mind. Others think of it in terms of training, in the sense of mental gymnastics. But meditation is neither of these, although it does involve dealing with neurotic states of mind. The neurotic state of mind is not difficult or impossible to deal with. It has energy, speed, and a certain pattern. The practice of meditation involves letting be—trying to go with the pattern, trying to go with the energy and the speed. In this way we learn how to deal with these factors, how to relate with them, not in the sense of causing them to mature in the way we would like, but in the sense of knowing them for what they are and working with their pattern.

17

Self-Truth

If you have any doubt about whether you're doing the meditation practice right or wrong, it doesn't matter all that much. The main point is to have honesty within yourself. Just do what you think is best. That is called self-truth. If truth is understood by oneself, then you cannot be persecuted at all, karmically or any other way. You're doing your best, so what can go wrong? Cheer up and have a good time.

18

Eliminating Unnecessary Complications

SHILA, OR DISCIPLINE, is the process of simplifying one's general life and eliminating unnecessary complications. In order to develop a genuine mental discipline, it is first necessary to see how we continually burden ourselves with extraneous activities and preoccupations. In Buddhist countries, shila might involve following a particular rule of life as a monk or a nun, or adopting the precepts appropriate to a Buddhist layperson. In the Western secular context, shila might just involve cultivating an attitude of simplicity toward one's life in general.

19

Crazy Monkey Mind

THE MIND is like a crazy monkey, which leaps about and never stays in one place. It is completely restless and constantly paranoid about its surroundings. The training, or the meditation practice, is a way to catch the monkey, to begin with. That is the starting point. Traditionally, this training is called *shamatha* in Sanskrit, or *shi-ne* in Tibetan, which means simply "the development of peace." When we talk about the development of peace, we are not talking about cultivating a peaceful state, as such, but about simplicity.

20

No Ambition

In true meditation, there is no ambition to stir up thoughts, nor is there an ambition to suppress them. They are just allowed to occur spontaneously and become an expression of basic sanity. They become the expression of the precision and the clarity of the awakened state of mind.

21

The Heart of the Buddha

HERE IS the really good news: We are intrinsically buddha, or intrinsically awake, and we are intrinsically good. Without exception, and without the need for analytical studies, we can say that we automatically have buddha within us. That is known as buddha-nature or *bodhichitta,* the heart of the Buddha.

22

Going beyond Fear

TRUE FEARLESSNESS is not the reduction of fear, but going beyond fear. Unfortunately, in the English language, we don't have one word that means that. Fearlessness is the closest term, but by fear*less* we don't mean "less fear," but "beyond fear." Going beyond fear begins when we examine our fear: our anxiety, nervousness, concern, and restlessness. If we look into our fear, if we look beneath its veneer, the first thing we find is sadness, beneath the nervousness. Nervousness is cranking up, vibrating, all the time. When we slow down, when we relax with our fear, we find sadness, which is calm and gentle. Sadness hits you in your heart, and your body produces a tear. Before you cry, there is a feeling in your chest and then, after that, you produce tears in your eyes. You are about to produce rain or a waterfall in your eyes, and you feel sad and lonely, and perhaps romantic at the same time. That is the first tip of fearlessness and the first sign of real warriorship. You might think that when you experience fearlessness you will hear the opening to Beethoven's Fifth Symphony or see a great explosion in the sky, but it doesn't happen that way. In the Shambhala tradition, discovering fearlessness comes from working with the softness of the human heart.

23

Phew!

Shamatha meditation practice is the development of mindfulness, paying attention to what is happening. Mainly this is working with your breath, your ordinary breathing. For example, if you've been exerting yourself, when you sit down to rest, you pay attention to your breathing. You walk toward your place of relaxation, and then, as you sit down, you say "phew." Breathing plays a very important part in ordinary common experience. Natural breathing, natural situations: that is the first thing that we can touch in terms of relaxation and peace.

24

The Greater Vision of Compassion

TAKING THE mahayana approach of benevolence means giving up privacy and developing a sense of greater vision. Rather than focusing on our own little projects, we expand our vision immensely to embrace working with the rest of the world, the rest of the galaxies, the rest of the universes. Putting such broad vision into practice requires that we relate to situations very clearly and perfectly.

In order to drop our self-centeredness, which both limits our view and clouds our actions, it is necessary for us to develop a sense of compassion. Traditionally this is done by first developing compassion toward oneself, then toward someone very close to us, and finally toward all sentient beings, including our enemies. Ultimately we regard all sentient beings with as much emotional involvement as if they were our own mothers. We may not require such a traditional approach at this point, but we can develop some sense of ongoing openness and gentleness.

25

Beyond Good and Bad

TRUE SPIRITUALITY is not a battle; it is the ultimate practice of nonviolence. We are not regarding any part of us as being a villain, an enemy, but we are trying to use everything as a part of the natural process of life. As soon as a notion of polarity, of good and bad develops, then we are caught in spiritual materialism, which is working to achieve happiness in a simple-minded sense, on the way to egohood.

26

Make Friends with Yourself

We get angry with ourselves, saying, "I could do better than this. What's wrong with me? I seem to be getting worse. I'm going backward." We're angry at the whole world, including ourselves. Everything we see is an insult. The universe becomes the expression of total insult. One has to relate with that. If you are going to exert your power and energy to walk on the path, you have to work with yourself. The first step is to make friends with yourself. That is almost the motto of *shamatha* or mindfulness meditation experience. Making friends with yourself means accepting and acknowledging yourself. You work with your subconscious gossip, fantasies, dreams—everything. And everything that you learn about yourself you bring back to the technique, to the awareness of the breathing, which was taught by the Buddha.

27

The Lion's Roar

THE LION'S ROAR is the fearless proclamation that any state of mind, including the emotions, is a workable situation, a reminder in the practice of meditation. We realize that chaotic situations must not be rejected. Nor should we regard them as regressive, as a return to confusion. We must respect whatever happens in our state of mind. Chaos should be regarded as extremely good news.

28

Arouse Your Sense of Wakefulness

In the fundamental sense, Buddhist meditation does not involve meditating on anything. You simply arouse your sense of wakefulness and hold an excellent posture. You hold up your head and shoulders and sit cross-legged. Then very simply, you relate to the basic notion of body, speech, and mind, and you focus your awareness in some way, usually using the breath. You are breathing out and in, and you just experience that breathing very naturally. Your breath is not considered either holy or evil; it is just breath.

29

The Boredom of Mountains and Waterfalls

Boredom is important in meditation practice; it increases the psychological sophistication of the practitioners. They begin to appreciate boredom and they develop their sophistication until the boredom begins to become cool boredom, like a mountain river. It flows and flows and flows, methodically and repetitiously, but it is very cooling, very refreshing. Mountains never get tired of being mountains, and waterfalls never get tired of being waterfalls. Because of their patience we begin to appreciate them. There is something in that. If we are to save ourselves from spiritual materialism and from *buddhadharma* with credentials, or dogma, if we are to become the dharma without credentials, the introduction of boredom and repetitiousness is extremely important.

30

Why Bother?

THIS LIFE is very valuable. Human birth is very important. You have a chance to practice, a chance to learn the truth, and still the question of "Why bother?" keeps cropping up again and again. You see, the path actually consists of "Who am I? What am I? What is this? What isn't this?" all the time until enlightenment is actually achieved. The question "Why bother?" has never been answered. It becomes one of the mantras of the path. "Why bother?" goes on all the time.

31

The Truth of Suffering

We must work with our fears, frustrations, disappointments, and irritations, the painful aspects of life. People complain that Buddhism is an extremely gloomy religion because it emphasizes suffering and misery. Usually religions speak of beauty, song, ecstasy, bliss. But according to Buddha, we must begin by seeing the experience of life as it is. We must see the truth of suffering, the reality of dissatisfaction. We cannot ignore it and attempt to examine only the glorious, pleasurable aspects of life. If one searches for a promised land, a Treasure Island, then the search only leads to more pain. So all sects and schools of Buddhism agree that we must begin by facing the reality of our living situations. We cannot begin by dreaming.

32

Absorb the Blame

EVEN THOUGH somebody else has made a terrible boo-boo and blamed it on you, you should take the blame yourself. You can actually say: "Okay, the blame is mine." Once you begin to do that, it is the highest and most powerful logic, the most powerful incantation you can make. You can absorb the poison—then the rest of the situation becomes medicine. If nobody is willing to absorb the blame, it becomes a big international football. Everybody tries to pass it on to each other and nothing happens. As far as international politics is concerned, somebody is always trying to put the blame on somebody else, to pass that huge, overbuilt, gooey, dirty, smelly, gigantic football with all sort of worms coming out of it. People say, "It's not mine, it's yours." So even from the point of view of political theory—if there is such a thing as politics in Buddhism—it is important for individuals to absorb unjustified blame and to work with that. It is very important and necessary.

33

When the Sun Rises

THE TRADITION of Shambhala is like the rising of the sun. When the sun rises, everybody is able to see it. But if people are blind, then they are not able to see it. When we say "blind," we are referring to the setting-sun people, those who do not connect with wakefulness. However, the fundamental or ultimate sun lies in the hearts of all people.

Therefore, everyone possesses fundamental well-being, brilliance, and purity. Whoever a person is, he or she is capable of crying, and also capable of laughing. That is the indication that everyone has the Great Eastern Sun within them.

34

Basic Sanity

IN CONTRAST to the traditional medical model of disturbances, the Buddhist approach is founded on the belief that basic sanity is operative in all states of mind. Confusion, from this point of view, is two-sided: it creates a need, a demand for sanity. This hungry nature of confusion is very powerful and very important. The demand for relief or sanity that is contained in confusion is, in fact, the beginning point of Buddhism. That is what moved Buddha to sit beneath the bodhi tree twenty-five hundred years ago—to confront his confusion and find its source—after struggling vainly for seven years in various ascetic yogic disciplines.

Basically, we are faced with a similar situation now in the West. Like Siddhartha before he became the Buddha, we are confused, anxious, and hungry psychologically. Despite a physically luxurious prosperity, there is a tremendous amount of emotional anxiety. This anxiety has stimulated a lot of research into various types of psychotherapy, drug therapy, behavior modification, and group therapies. From the Buddhist viewpoint, this search is evidence of the nature of basic sanity operating within neurosis.

35

True Spirituality

SPIRITUALITY does not exist on another level, or on a "higher plane," quite different from ordinary life, as is generally assumed. It is no use trying to be different than you are. Spirituality is not about trying to be something more than you are or something better than you are, for that matter. What is known as relative truth, or the truth which exists right here, now, in our everyday life, that truth has to be accepted as the general ground, and it is also the absolute truth.

36

Money

Money is basically a very simple thing. But our attitude toward it is overloaded, full of preconceived ideas that stem from the development of a self-aggrandizing ego and its manipulative processes. The mere act of handling money—just pieces of paper—is viewed as a very serious game. The energy money takes on makes a tremendous difference in the process of communication and relationship. If a friend suddenly refuses to pay his check at a restaurant, a feeling of resentment or separation automatically arises in relation to him. If one buys a friend a cup of tea—which is just a cup, hot water, and tea—somehow a factor of meaningfulness gets added.

It seems to me that it is worthwhile to work with the negative aspects of money in order to gain some understanding about ourselves. We must try to discover how to view this embarrassing and potent commodity as a part of ourselves that we cannot ignore. When we relate to money properly, it is no longer a mere token of exchange or of our abstract energy; it is also a discipline. Then we can deal with it in a practical, earthy way as a master deals with his tools.

37

Real Kindness

THE TERM *MAITRI,* loving-kindness, or even compassion, is generally rather sentimental and weak in the English language. It has certain connotations connected with the popular concept of charity and being kind to our neighbors. The real concept of maitri is different from that. In part, of course, it does involve a sentimental approach, since there is always room for the emotions. However, maitri is not just being kind and nice. It is the understanding that one has to become one with the situation. That does not mean that one becomes entirely without personality and has to just accept whatever the other person suggests. Rather, one has to overcome the barrier that one has formed between oneself and others. If you remove this barrier and open yourself, then automatically real understanding and clarity will develop in your mind.

38

Energy Is a Powerful Teacher

THE HAPPENINGS OF LIFE are manifestations of energy. This energy in the situations of life is a very powerful teacher. If you go too far, in the sense of not being receptive enough to learn from the experience of life, if you ignore this experience and go too far with the extreme emotional excitement of ego, then sooner or later you are going to be pulled back. This might take the form of accident, illness, or disaster—any sort of chaos. Whereas if you are able to see the first signal that you have lost touch with the life situation as teacher, then you will be able to tune yourself back into it. That is "guru-as-environment."

39

The Body

THE BODY doesn't have to be special. The whole world is your body. There's a tendency to view the body as your private possession. And because of that, you tend to forget the rest of the world and the greater orbit of experience involved with that. If a person is able to relate with the world, he is also able to relate with the body. And if a person is able to relate with the body thoroughly, then that person also would learn how to open to the world.

40

Being a Person of Sanity

It is through body, speech, and mind that we relate with the phenomenal world. Such a relationship is not necessarily spiritual; it is physical, bodily. It is a question of being a person of sanity, a person of openness. In fact, we could almost approach the whole path in a secular way and call it the nontheistic discipline of developing sanity and openness, rather than regarding it as purely a religious tradition.

41

A Great Feast

ONE OF THE PROBLEMS we have is that, in relating with the samsaric, confused emotions, we behave like misers; we are too frugal. We feel that we have something to lose and something to gain, so we work with the emotions just pinch by pinch. But when we work on the wisdom level, we think in terms of greater emotions: greater anger, greater passion, greater speed; therefore, we begin to lose our ground and our boundaries. Then we have nothing to fight for. Everything is our world, so what is the point of fighting? What is the point of segregating things in terms of this and that? The whole thing becomes a larger-scale affair, and ego's territory seems very cheap, almost inapplicable or nonexistent. That is why tantra is called a great feast.

42

Open Faith

Personal openness is the important thing, rather than purely living on faith. Faith can be blind or intelligent. Open faith is intelligent, being willing to include one's confusion and one's understanding at the same time. Blind faith is purely going by facts and figures, thinking in terms of quick results, depending on fame, reputation, and so forth. It is like saying you should read a book because this book is a best seller. Five million copies have been sold, therefore it must be good. It is possible that five million stupid people bought it and read it. But that's the kind of reference point of blind faith.

43

A Glimpse of Buddha Nature

A GLIMPSE of buddha nature is not a glimpse in the sense of viewing something: it is a gap rather than a glimpse. That gap is the experience that comes out of seeing through the veils of ego. But whether we have a glimpse of it or not, the buddha mind is still functioning in us all the time. It occurs in the most bizarre, cheap, and confused styles we might present, as well as in whatever extremely profound, dignified, and wise experiences we might have. All of those are the expressions of buddha nature.

44

The Purpose of Work

WORK CAN BE regarded as not having any purpose behind it at all. Instead, it is just work for the sake of working. You can experience ignorance or happiness without it being ignorance *of* something or happiness *about* something. Likewise, work does not need an object. You don't have to have a particular aim, object, goal, or moralistic sense of discipline. You just work because you work. You simply relate with your physical being or your sense of existence as part of the work process, which also brings communication with the actual realistic living world.

45

Constant Discipline

DISCIPLINE IS NOT a one-shot deal or a two-shot deal, but a one-hundred-thousand shot deal. It happens again and again and again. Discipline is not somebody with a long face and a stick. Discipline is somebody without a face, without a stick—but cool, cold, fifty degrees below zero. Discipline is not a schoolmaster or a Zen master with a stick in *zazen* practice or a disciplinarian or an angry, hot-tempered tutor. Discipline is not a person at all. That makes it hard to relate with, because you can't rebel against it. You can't take the stick away from the disciplinarian and hit him back. It's constant discipline. Cool mountain stream. It's very boring. So let's call it cool boredom. The boredom which such discipline consists of is cool boredom, refreshing boredom.

46

Greater Vision

WE PREFER to wear sunglasses, rather than facing the brilliance of the sunshine. We put on a hat and sunscreen to shield ourselves, fearing that we might get burned. The colorfulness of relationships, household chores, business enterprises, and our general livelihood are too irritating. We are constantly looking for padding so that we don't run into the sharp edges of the world. That is the essence of wrong belief. It is an obstacle to seeing the wisdom of the Great Eastern Sun, which is seeing greater vision beyond our own small world.

47

Hearing Words of Wisdom

WHEN WE LISTEN to a speaker, we are gathered and expectant. We expect an ideal message or certain edifying ideas from the speaker. Because of our need to satisfy our intellect and emotions and to get some security, we want to hear words of wisdom, and we remold the speaker's words to satisfy that need. We shape them and reshape them, manufacturing fixed and definite impressions from the raw materials of the speaker's words. The result is that we constantly have nothing but ourselves bouncing back on ourselves. That is always a problem. It is very difficult to find both an audience who will sit in no-man's-land and a speaker who speaks from no-man's-land. That kind of attitude is very difficult, extremely hard to find.

48

The Future Is Virgin Territory

The preservation of the past in the present is called memory. We have developed all those memories as possible ways of solidifying our existence. Whenever we experience a loss of feeling or a loss of inspiration, we constantly refer back to that habitual pattern, which brings us some kind of outdated information. We then try to adapt that outdated information to the up-to-date situation, which is a manipulation of the anxiety of the present state. That whole process is what's called "karmic creation." But this process doesn't go on into the future at all. The future is a virgin situation, completely unoccupied territory. We can't manipulate the future because nothing has happened in the future so far—so the future is a completely open situation.

49

Learning to Wake Up

We are hungry for knowledge and want to get results immediately and automatically, but unless we give up that speed and urgency, we are not going to learn anything. The problem seems to be basically one of laziness. We are so lazy that we do not even want to bother eating our food; we would prefer to be satisfied just from reading the menu. And that laziness reaches the extreme when it comes to going further into relating with reality. The process of learning to wake up takes time and painful measures of all kinds. The learning process is not an easy matter. It is not easy, because we do not want to surrender our basic security. The teachings of Buddhism are not a source of security, such as "the freedom of nirvana" or something of that nature. The teachings do not present another form of security at all, but bring the absence of any kind of security. Enlightenment is the complete absence of any kind of promises.

50

Working with Pain

When there is physical pain, there is also a kind of mental irritation connected with it. And this mental irritation, this "pain," is something we build up unnecessarily with the hope of getting rid of the physical pain. In fact, this produces even more pain. Pain may make us feel that we are shut in, that we are helpless, that we have to contact the doctor, that we have to have medicine, that we have to do something about our pain. So there is a continual search for relief, a running after something, rather than first just examining, questioning, seeing pain for what it is. "Where did this pain come from?" "What actually is it?" When a person is able to see with faith in oneself, rather than asking for help all the time, perhaps then one might do something to help oneself. Until one develops that kind of self-confidence and understanding of the positive element in oneself and one's experience, it is very difficult to see the true pattern of relative truth, which also contains the absolute.

Perhaps after a certain incident, you find your whole pattern of life changed: through an accident, a severe illness, or going through a war, you realize that there is something profound happening. When one no longer thinks of the pain as something separate from oneself, then one finds something familiar in it, something to be learned from it. In this way, suffering acts as a vehicle, and one realizes that there is a positive element in it.

51

Basic Goodness

EVERYBODY possesses the unconditioned possibility of cheerfulness, which is not connected purely with either pain or pleasure. You have an inclination: in the flash of one second, you feel what needs to be done. It is not a product of your education; it is not scientific or logical; you simply pick up on the message. And then you act: you just do it. That basic human quality of suddenly opening up is the best part of human instinct. You know what to do right away, on the spot—which is fantastic. That is what we call the dot of basic goodness and unconditional instinct. You don't think: you just feel, on the spot. Basic trust is knowing that there is such a thing as that spark of basic goodness. Although you might be in the worst of the worst shape, still that goodness does exist.

52

Click into the Sense of Delight

THE PHENOMENAL WORLD is self-existing. You can see it, you can look at it, you can appreciate your survey, and you can present your view to others. It is possible to discover the inherent state of things. It is possible to perceive how the world hangs together. It is possible to communicate your appreciation to others. The possibility of freshness is always there. Your mind is never totally contaminated by your neuroses. Goodness is always there. Catch it on the spot. Click into the sense of delight that comes from basic wakefulness.

53

The Golden Chain of Spirituality

As long as we follow a spiritual approach promising salvation, miracles, liberation, then we are bound by the "golden chain of spirituality." Such a chain might be beautiful to wear, with its inlaid jewels and intricate carvings, but nevertheless, it imprisons us. People think they can wear the golden chain for decoration without being imprisoned by it, but they are deceiving themselves. As long as one's approach to spirituality is based upon enriching ego, then it is spiritual materialism, a suicidal process rather than a creative one.

54

Secular Enlightenment

In Tibet, as well as many other Asian countries, there are stories about a legendary kingdom that was a place of peace and prosperity, governed by wise and compassionate rulers. The citizens were equally kind and learned, so that, in general, the kingdom was a model society. This place was called Shambhala. Among many Tibetan Buddhist teachers, there has long been a tradition that regards the kingdom of Shambhala not as an external place but as the ground or root of wakefulness and sanity that exists as a potential within every human being. From that point of view, it is not important to decide whether the kingdom of Shambhala is fact or fiction. Instead, we should appreciate and emulate the ideal of an enlightened society that it represents. The Shambhala teachings use the image of the Shambhala kingdom to represent the ideal of secular enlightenment, that is, the possibility of uplifting our personal existence and that of others without the need for any religious outlook. With the great problems now facing human society, it seems increasingly important to find simple and nonsectarian ways to work with ourselves and to share our understanding with others.

55

Success and Failure

TRUST IS BEING WILLING to take a chance, knowing that what goes up must come down, as they say. When a warrior has that kind of trust in the reflections of the phenomenal world, then she can trust her individual discovery of goodness. Communication produces results, either success or failure. That is how the fearless warrior relates with the universe: not by remaining alone and insecure, hiding away, but by constantly being exposed to the phenomenal world and constantly being willing to take that chance.

The ancient Chinese *Book of Changes* or *I Ching* often talks about success being failure and failure being success. Success sows the seeds of future failure, and failure may bring a later success. So it's always a dynamic process. As warriors, fearlessness doesn't mean that we cheer up by saying, "Look! I'm on the side of the right. I'm a success." Nor do we feel that we're being punished when we fail. In either case, success and failure are saying the same thing.

56

Make Friends with Fear

IN ORDER to understand the notion of fearlessness, one has to understand fear itself. Fear is a trembling, shaky feeling of being afraid of nonexistence. Such fear is not necessarily regarded as problematic. It is like an attack of sneezing. But you have to study your fear, definitely: how it arises, how it manifests, and how it is actualized. When you begin to understand such fear, then you begin to find that it is almost a big joke. But you shouldn't try to cast fear out. Fear should be regarded as the kindling you use to build a big fire of fearlessness. So you have to understand fear as the starting point of fearlessness. Fear is not regarded as black, and fearlessness is not regarded as white. You have to make friends with fear.

57

Advice to Psychologists

THE MAIN POINT in working with people is to appreciate and manifest simplicity rather than trying to create new theories or categories of behavior. The more you appreciate simplicity, the more profound your understanding becomes. Simplicity begins to make much more sense than speculation.

58

Fresh Dharma

THE TEACHINGS are an individual personal experience, right down to the present holder of the lineage. They have the quality of warm, fresh baked bread; the bread is still warm and hot and fresh. Each baker must apply the general knowledge of how to make bread to his particular dough and oven. Then he must personally experience the freshness of this bread and must cut it fresh and eat it warm. It is a very living process. There is no deception in terms of viewing the teachings as collecting knowledge. We must work with our individual experiences. When we become confused, we cannot turn back to our collection of knowledge and try to find some confirmation or consolation: "The teacher and the whole teaching are on my side." The spiritual path does not go that way. It is a lonely individual path.

59

Patience without Expectations

One should not expect anything from outside. One should not try to change the other person or try to put across one's opinions. One should not try to convince a person at the wrong moment, when one knows he already has a very clear idea of his own, or it is simply not the right moment for your words to get through to him. There is an analogy of two people walking barefoot along a very rough road, and one thought it would be very good to cover the whole road with leather, so it would be very soft, but the other one, who was wiser, said, "No, I think if we covered our feet with leather that would be the same." So that is patience, which is not being distrustful, but is a matter of not expecting anything and not trying to change the situation outside oneself. And that is the only way to create peace in the world.

60

The Echo Chamber

USUALLY WHEN things go wrong, we come up with an excuse. But blame doesn't come from one's partners or friends. Taking blame onto yourself means that it is *yours.* In other words, when you're outside and you shout something, if it bounces off a rock, then the rock says, "ai, ai, ai, ai." But you don't blame the rock. You blame yourself, because *you* said "ai, ai, ai, ai." You're in an echo chamber, so you blame the echo*er,* rather than the echo itself. Therefore there is hope; there is hope of reducing blame. That is true blamelessness.

61

Contacting Reality

Spirituality is simply a means of arousing one's spirit, of developing a kind of spiritedness. Through that you begin to have greater contact with reality. You are not afraid of discovering what reality is all about, and you are willing to explore your individual energy. You actually choose to work with the essence of your existence, which could be called genuineness. An interest in spirituality doesn't mean that you lack something, or that you have developed a black hole in your existence which you are trying to compensate for or cover over with some sort of religious patchwork. It simply means that you are capable of dealing with reality.

62

The Smile of Shambhala

EVEN IN THE DARKEST of the Dark Age, there is always light. That light comes with a smile, the smile of Shambhala, the smile of fearlessness, the smile of realizing the best of the best of human potential.

63

Leap of Daring

In order to overcome selfishness, it is necessary to be daring. It is as though you were dressed in your swimsuit, standing on the diving board with a pool in front of you, and you asked yourself: "Now what?" The obvious answer is: "Jump." That is daring. You might wonder if you will sink or hurt yourself if you jump. You might. There is no insurance, but it is worthwhile jumping to find out what will happen. The student warrior has to jump. We are so accustomed to accepting what is bad for us and rejecting what is good for us. We are attracted to our cocoons, our selfishness, and we are afraid of selflessness, stepping beyond ourselves. So in order to overcome our hesitation about giving up our privacy, and in order to commit ourselves to others' welfare, some kind of leap is necessary.

64

Audible Silence

IN ORDER to achieve silence, you don't have to chase the birds away because they're making noise. In order to be still, you don't have to stop the movement of air or the rushing river. If you accept them, you will yourself be aware of the silence. Just accept them as part of the establishment of silence. The noise that birds make is one factor, and one's psychological concept of noise is another. And when one can deal with that side, the noise of birds becomes merely audible silence.

65

Learning the Art of War

In order to successfully challenge someone, first of all you must develop loving-kindness and a feeling of longing for openness, so that there is no desire to challenge anyone at all. If one has a desire to conquer or win a challenge against another, then in the process of challenging him or her, the mind is filled with this desire and one is not really able to challenge the other properly. Going beyond challenge is learning the art of war. In the Chinese, Tibetan, and Japanese traditions, real warriors do not think in terms of challenge, nor are their minds occupied with the battlefield or with past or future consequences. The warrior is completely one with bravery, one with that particular moment. You are fully concentrated in the moment, because you know the art of war. You are entirely skilled in your tactics: you do not refer to past events or develop your strength through thinking about future consequences and victory. You are fully aware at that moment, which automatically brings success in the challenge.

66

The Future Is in Our Hands

We hold the threshold of the future of the world in our hands, on our path. When we say this, we are not dreaming. We are not exaggerating. We hold a tremendous hope, maybe the only hope for the future dark age.

We have a lot of responsibilities, and those responsibilities are not easy to fulfill. They won't come along easily, like an ordinary success story. They have to be stitched, painted, carved, step by step, inch by inch, minute by minute. It will be manual work. There will be no automatic big sweep, or solution.

When something good is done in the world, it is usually difficult. It is manual, rather than automatic. When something bad is done, usually that is automatic. Evil things are easy to catch, but good ones are difficult to catch. They go against the grain of ordinary habitual tendencies.

67

The Meaning of Life

ALL OF US are concerned with discovering the meaning of life. Some people say that the meaning of life is found only in spiritual practice, and some people say it is found only in human dignity. From some, the meaning of life is becoming a successful person. So the meaning of life is under dispute, subject to philosophical struggle and metaphysical doubts. What really is the meaning of life? The question still remains. We do not know. The meaning of life is uncertain.

We have something in common, you and I: we are baffled by the meaning of life. I could make up some things, but I feel that is not a particularly kind thing to do. We are at a loss. Yet, quite possibly, we don't have to solve the problem of the meaning of life, as such. We could start on something else we have in common. That is confusion. We are completely baffled. We could start from there.

68

Misunderstanding Freedom

THERE SEEMS TO BE some misunderstanding of the idea of freedom. We think we will be entertained by freedom, rather than actually being a free person, spiritually speaking. You feel that you could indulge in freedom, which automatically means bondage. You depend on freedom for your happiness. You think that, once you are free, you could indulge in spiritual achievement. You could see the future; you could see the past. You will have telepathic powers and read people's minds. You will have power over others. You could wipe out pain, disregarding karmic situations. You could take over the whole world! That is the spiritual idea of materialism.

69

Awareness of Mind

THE *SHAMATHA* style of meditation, meditation based on mindfulness, is particularly recommended by the Buddha. It has been known as the only way for beginning meditators for 2,500 years. To begin with, we could discuss the attitude that brings about possibilities of mindfulness. This attitude is not particularly opinionated. When we talk about attitude in this context, we are talking about awareness of mind, which is precisely what mindfulness is. Awareness of mind means that you are aware, that your mind is aware of yourself. In other words, the basic point is that you're aware that you're aware. The suggestion here is that you are not a machine; you are an individual person relating with what's happening around you. And mindfulness in this particular case is the sense of being.

70

Developing Fearless Renunciation

THE GROUND of fearlessness and the basis of overcoming doubt and wrong belief is to develop renunciation. Renunciation here means overcoming that very hard, tough, aggressive mentality that wards off any gentleness that might come into our hearts. Fear does not allow fundamental tenderness to enter into us. When tenderness tinged by sadness touches our heart, we know that we are in contact with reality. We feel it. That contact is genuine, fresh, and quite raw. That sensitivity is the basic experience of warriorship, and it is the key to developing fearless renunciation.

71

Meditation Is the Only Way

If you saw two rocks sticking out of the ocean, they might appear to be different from one another on the surface, but if you dove underneath to the seabed, then you might find they were both part of a huge, giant, great rock. So all spirituality in the West and in the East is based on the practice of meditation.

Meditation is the only way to link not only East and West but, perhaps, the whole world, the whole universe. Meditation is the only way that links and that introduces spirituality, and that could make things real and enable people to really see the I-less state—egolessness. Meditation is the only way to see the profound meaning of *duhkha*—suffering. Meditation is the only way to see the profound meaning of life. It could be switching out a light or pouring out a cup of tea, but there is a great symbol, a great depth of meaning in this, which can only be reached through meditation.

72

Perfect Actors

THERE ARE enormous problems with thinking that we can only trust in what we are told rather than in how we feel. When we have only been *told* how to handle ourselves, our behavior can become automatic. Automatically we pick and choose. We learn to be perfect actors. It does not matter how we feel. We might be in tears, but still we put on a gleaming smile and make polite conversation. If we cannot find anything good to talk about, we just talk about the weather. With that approach, we become very crude. In fact, we are trying to become perfect actors rather than real people.

73

Tricky Warriors

We don't want to become tricky warriors, with all kinds of tricks up our sleeves and ways to cut people's logic down when we don't agree with them. Then there is no cultivation of either ourselves or others. When that occurs, we destroy any possibilities of enlightened society. In fact, there will be no society; just a few people hanging out. Instead, the fearless warriors of Shambhala are very ordinary, simple-minded warriors. That is the starting point for developing true bravery.

74

The Buddhist Journey

The Buddhist journey is a journey from beginning to end in which the end is also the beginning. Once you get onto this particular bandwagon, it is an ongoing journey without reverse and without brakes. It is an ongoing process. Beginning this journey is committing yourself to a particular karmic flow, a karmic chain reaction. It is like being born. When you are born, nobody can say, "That was just a rehearsal" and take the whole thing back. Once you are born, you keep on growing up, growing older, becoming aged, more aged, and then finally you die. When you are born, there is a certain amount of commitment involved—to be born as a human child from a mother's womb, with parents, with a house, and so on. This Buddhist journey is a very definite one, absolutely definite, and that is why it is called Buddhism. Although "-ism" is a rather ugly suffix, it is a definite "-ism." It is a "Buddha-ism," because we are trying to imitate Buddha's journey.

75

Accepting Imperfections

WE MUST BE WILLING to be completely ordinary people, which means accepting ourselves as we are without trying to become greater, purer, more spiritual, more insightful. If we can accept our imperfections as they are, quite ordinarily, then we can use them as part of the path. But if we try to get rid of our imperfections, then they will be enemies, obstacles on the road to our "self-improvement." And the same is true for the breath in meditation. If we can see it as it is, without trying to use it to improve ourselves, then it becomes a part of the path because we are no longer using it as the tool of our personal ambition.

76

Beyond Effort

When performing meditation practice one should think of it as just a natural function of everyday life, like eating or breathing, not as a special, formal event to be undertaken with great seriousness and solemnity. One must realize that to meditate is to pass beyond effort, beyond practice, beyond aims and goals, and beyond the dualism of bondage and liberation.

77
Early-Morning Depression

WHEN YOU FEEL depressed, it is sometimes for no reason at all. You wake up in the morning and feel hopeless, terrible. We may justify that feeling, saying I feel bad . . . because I don't have any money. I feel bad . . . because something has gone wrong in my life. In fact, our early-morning depression is not all that logical. It is the curse of the setting sun. Out of nowhere, you just don't feel so good. *Then* you come up with logical explanations for why you are depressed.

Everybody knows this fundamental depression. We do all sorts of things to avoid it: waiting for the arrival of the newspaper in the morning; even watching *Sesame Street* with or without our children. There are lots of aids to forget depression, and billions of dollars are spent on those attempts to cheer up.

In the Shambhala tradition, we talk about how fearlessness comes out of the realization of fear. Similarly, when you experience morning depression, it is possible to cheer up. From morning depression and its terror, we can step right into basic goodness. Our depression is like a wobbly staircase. When you put your foot on the first step, you wonder whether it will hold you. You might fall. But as you take further steps, you realize that it's going to carry you upstairs. We learn to reject the terror of morning depression and to step into morning basic goodness, right on the spot.

78

No Barriers

When a person is able to see what is *now* without being influenced by the past or any expectation of the future, but just seeing the very moment of now, then at that moment, there is no barrier at all. For a barrier could only arise from association with the past or expectation of the future. So the present moment has no barriers at all. A person finds there is a tremendous energy within himself, a tremendous strength to practice patience.

79

Wisdom Is Like Outer Space

JNANA IS A SANSKRIT word that literally means "primordial insight." That is to say, it is insight, understanding, clarity, oneness. Jnana is a state of discriminating wisdom that always occurs rather than being produced by temporary experience of any kind. It is an inherent state of being. So jnana is like outer space, which is inherently outer space. In spite of stars, moons, galaxies, and planets of all kinds, nevertheless, it is basic space. Outer space is inherently empty and inherently rich at the same time, like jnana, wisdom.

80

Eternally Rich

THE BASIC practice of richness is learning to project the goodness that exists in your being, so that a sense of goodness shines out. When you feel that your life is established properly and fully, you feel that a golden rain is continuously descending. It feels solid, simple, and straightforward. Then you also have a feeling of gentleness and openness, as though an exquisite flower has bloomed auspiciously in your life. Although at that particular point you might be penniless, there is no problem. You are suddenly, eternally rich.

81

The Feminine Principle

THE *DAKINI* or the feminine principle of energy is all-pervading energy within our state of mind. This energy manifests as either destructive or positive. It seems to describe the source of chaos in the world, whether there may be war or famine or the confusion in people's minds. Everything is caused by this dakini principle of energy, including positive aspects of situations as well. Therefore, dealing with this energy is very important in the practice of meditation as well as in life as a whole. One might regard oneself as completely law-abiding and sensible. But equally, there are other energy aspects creeping underneath that. One cannot simply try to be aware and watch oneself, do good, and be sensible; that is, try to be good. But one must also deal with one's own powerful energy flow, which could manifest as love, hate, jealousy, pride as well as other manifestations. They are not necessarily to be condemned.

82

Embarrassing Moments

In the *shamatha* or mindfulness approach to meditation practice, you don't just give yourself an easy time so you can escape the embarrassing and unpleasant moments, the self-conscious moments of your life. Such thoughts might arise as memories of the past, or the painful experiences of the present, or painful future prospects. All those things arise in your practice, and you experience them and look at them and let them come back to your breath. This is very important.

83

Ordinary Is Extraordinary

When you look up at the sky, if you see a blue sky, you don't quite accept it. You don't want to just look at the blue sky. You want to see clouds. We're always looking for something else. Still, the phenomenal world is filled with fantastic possibilities. You don't need to find extra ways to entertain yourself. It is a question of accepting and acknowledging things as they are, learning to accept the ordinariness of extraordinariness. The Shambhala approach is to befriend what is there, the everyday occurrence, which is real, obvious, and constant. It may be the same blue sky and the same Volkswagen car that we drive to work every day. But that ordinariness is extraordinary. That is the dichotomy: When you live life in a thoroughly ordinary way, it is extraordinary.

84

Grains of Sand

WE THINK we are great, broadly significant, and that we cover a whole large area. We see ourselves as having a history and a future, and here we are in our big-deal present. But if we look at ourselves clearly in this very moment, we see we are just grains of sand—just little people concerned only with this little dot which is called nowness.

85

Glimpse of Enlightenment

FUNDAMENTALLY the idea of enlightenment—the notion or term "enlightenment" or "buddha" or "awakened one"—implies tremendous sharpness and precision along with a sense of spaciousness. We can experience this; it is not myth at all. We experience a glimpse of it, and the point is to start from that glimpse and gradually, as you become more familiar with that glimpse and the possibilities of reigniting it, it happens naturally. There occurs a flash, maybe a fraction of a second. These flashes happen constantly, all the time. Faith is realizing that there is some open space and sharpness in your everyday life.

86

A Natural State of Awareness

Awareness does not mean be careful, ward off danger, you might step into a puddle, so beware. That is not the kind of awareness we are talking about. We are talking about unconditional presence, which is not expected to be there all the time. In fact, in order to be completely aware, you have to disown the experience of awareness. It cannot be regarded as yours—it is just there and you do not try to hold on to it. Then, somehow, a general clarity takes place. So awareness is a glimpse rather than a continuous state. If you hold on to awareness, it becomes self-consciousness rather than awareness. Awareness has to be unmanufactured; it has to be a natural state.

87

Buddha Genes

The heart of the Buddha is very open. That heart would like to explore the phenomenal world; it is open to relating with others. That heart contains tremendous strength and confidence in itself, which is called fearlessness. That heart is also extremely inquisitive, which at this point is synonymous with *prajna,* or discriminating awareness. It is expansive and sees in all directions. And that heart contains certain basic qualities, which we could call our true basic genes—our buddha genes. We all possess those particular buddha genes. Isn't it strange to say that the heart has genes? But it turns out to be true. These genes are ever so loving, which goes beyond just being kind. They are absolutely free from any form of aggression. They are so soft and kind.

88

Life Teaches Us

Every life situation teaches us something. If we go too fast, some incident takes place in our lives to slow us down. If we are going too slow, our lives begin to push us. Life situations always contain a message. And that message can be understood, to begin with, if we realize that life situations are providing us with the positive resources we need. They have nothing to do with destruction or original sin or any pain or misery—there's nothing that we have to reject. The process of learning spontaneously from our life situation seems to be the starting point.

89

Tradition

Tradition is not necessarily a system developed by anybody, but tradition is the natural understanding of things as they are, which is based on why we see—and everybody agrees—that the sky is blue and the grass is green. Tradition is that way, rather than anybody's established law and order or personal opinion of any kind. Therefore tradition is common sense at its best. Enlightenment is also the height of common sense. Therefore it is regarded as a tradition. It is also regarded as infallible, as true and powerful. It never can be contradicted. Nobody can say, "the sky is green" or "the grass is red." That basic logic—that hot is hot, cold is cold, daytime is light, nighttime is dark—is tradition. That is the truth and at the same time it is tradition.

90

Meditation Posture

There is a difference between animals and human beings. Many animals find relaxation while still standing on four legs. Horses can sleep that way. They could even meditate that way, if anybody taught horses to meditate. Snakes and lizards, horses and cows, could all meditate with their heads horizontal to the body. The head and body are one horizontal unit. But as far as human beings are concerned, we don't walk on four feet at this point in our evolution. We have no chance of going back, so we have to walk on our two feet. For us a vertical posture happens, with our heads higher than the rest of our body, including when we sit in meditation. So since we are formed this way, we should practice meditation this way. The Buddha set an example. The Buddha for human beings sits upright in the meditation posture. This isn't particularly anthropocentric, in the sense that human beings are regarded as the highest beings. It's a question of what our makeup is, and we should go along with our makeup. So posture in meditation is very important. It's upright as opposed to animal style, and not too tense in your neck. Just sit up, very simply.

91

The Spiritual Babysitter

USUALLY WE SAY that in theistic traditions you worship an external agent, and in nontheistic traditions you do not worship an external agent. Nonetheless, in either case you might just be looking for your version of a babysitter. Whether you hire a babysitter from the outside world or from within your own family doesn't really matter. In either case, your state of being isn't being expressed properly, thoroughly, because you are trying to use some kind of substitute. We are not trying here to sort out which tradition, or which particular type of merchandise, is better. We are talking in terms of needing to develop a personal connection with one's body and one's mind. That is why the contemplative traditions of both East and West are very important.

92

Spirituality without Materialism

In the spiritual materialistic approach, spirituality is regarded as bringing happiness. You say to yourself, "I could take off into the mountains and meditate in a cave. It will be a much simpler and more pleasurable life. I won't be bound by any obligations to anything at all. I won't have to answer the telephone. I won't have to maintain my house. I'll enjoy the fresh air. Meditation will come naturally, once there are no disturbances. There will be no one to irritate me, because I've abandoned those dirty associations from my past history. I won't care who I was, but I will care who I *am,* living in the mountains, enjoying the beauty of nature, the fresh air, and vibrations." However, something is uncertain or missing from this whole vision.

It has been said that compassion is important, as well as wisdom. Spirituality without spiritual materialism is an attitude of compassion. Finally, you have to return to the world. And not just finally, but you have to work with the world. You have to relate with the world, because enlightened mind contains both wisdom as well as compassion simultaneously. So you have an obligation to the world that brought you up, the world that you belong to.

93

Genuine Inspiration

GENUINE INSPIRATION is not particularly dramatic. It's very ordinary. It comes from settling down in your environment and accepting situations as natural. Out of that you begin to realize that you can dance with them. So inspiration comes from acceptance rather than from having a sudden flash of a good gimmick coming up in your mind. Inspiration has two parts: openness and clear vision, or in Sanskrit, *shunyata* and *prajna*. Both are based on the notion of original mind, traditionally known as buddha mind, which is blank, nonterritorial, noncompetitive, and open.

94

Disappointment

We might think that in the spiritual search we are simply concerned with fulfillment, happiness, accomplishment, and enlightenment. But at the same time the spiritual path requires some sacrifice, some act of generosity, some kind of training before we reach happiness and goodness. Therefore, the idea of disappointment plays an important role. In this case "disappointment" means we cannot fulfill every expectation of ego, nor can we achieve everything that we want to achieve without any giving or any openness. In other words, disappointment means that we cannot become self-made buddhas. We have to experience the reality of life as such before we can decide to proclaim ourselves to be enlightened.

95

A Constant Unmasking

Treading on the spiritual path, according to the Buddha, is not a pleasurable situation, neither is it a blissful one. In the lives of great teachers in the past, it was a constant unmasking, a constant giving away, a constant undressing, peeling off skin after skin, layer after layer, mask after mask. Getting on the spiritual path is like getting into a vehicle without brakes. Traditionally, it is said that it would be better not to begin such a trip, but if we must begin such a journey, we should prepare for it and we should not expect bliss as soon as we start out. Bliss, pleasure, and joy should emanate from some kind of work, some kind of sacrifice, some kind of giving in.

96

The Path Includes Everything

Aggression is very deep rooted. Anger is like the heart of the earth: It has brewed for years and years and years, thousands of years. And when it is just about to give a little peep out on the surface of the earth, that is aggression. Don't try to make it go away, and don't try to invite it—that is what's called the path. The path consists of collections of dirt, stones, grasses. It includes everything—passion, aggression, and ignorance. Without those, you have no path. So you shouldn't try to build a highway and have everything smooth under your car. That's the difference between the Buddhist path and the American materialistic path.

97

We Are Indebted

We can't give up the world all together and disassociate ourselves from the past or from that which irritates us. In fact, compassion is the only way. It is what brings us back to the world. We have to work with people. We have to work with our fathers, our mothers, our sisters, our brothers, our neighbors, and our friends. We have to work with them. We have to relate with them. Those who are our relations, who represent our relationships or our associations with life situations, are the only inspiration. They inspired us to undertake a spiritual search. Without them, we wouldn't be able to look into spirituality at all. These people provide irritation, negativity, aggression, demands, etc. They provide everything to us. Because their kindness and their energy inspired us, therefore we are indebted to work with them.

98

Unconditional Cheerfulness

Transplanting the moon of wakefulness into your heart and the sun of wisdom into your head can be natural and obvious. It is not so much trying to look for the bright side of life and using that side of things as a stepping-stone, but it is discovering unconditional cheerfulness, which has no other side. It is just one side, one taste. From that, the natural sense of goodness begins to dawn in your heart. Therefore, whatever we experience, whatever we see, whatever we hear, whatever we think—all those activities begin to have some sense of holiness or sacredness in them. The world is full of hospitality at that point. Sharp corners begin to dissolve and the darkness begins to be uplifted in our lives. That kind of goodness is unconditionally good, and at that point, we become a decent human being and a warrior. Such an approach has to be accompanied by the sitting practice of meditation. The practice of meditation acts as a training ground and stronghold. Out of that, the seed of friendliness begins to occur. The main point is to appreciate your world. That kind of world is known as the *vajra,* or indestructible, world. It is a cheerful world. It never becomes too good or too bad.

99

Grain of Sand, Emperor of the Universe

If we begin to realize that we are purely grains of sand, specks of dust in the midst of the universe, then the universe becomes inviting and inspiring. If we are grains of sand, then the rest of the universe, all of space, all the room that there is, is ours, because we are not obstructing anything other than our one grain of sand. Because we are grains of sand, there is tremendous openness. Each of us is the emperor of the universe, the conqueror of the whole universe. We each become the *chakravartin,* the universal monarch, simply because we are grains of sand.

100

Nonexistence

NONEXISTENCE is the only preparation for tantra, the highest teachings of Buddhism, and we should realize that there is no substitute. The experience of nonexistence brings a sense of delightful humor and, at the same time, complete openness and freedom. In addition, it brings an experience of complete indestructibility that is unchallengeable, immovable, and completely solid. The experience of indestructibility can only occur when we realize that nonexistence is possible, in the sense of being without reference points, without philosophical definitions, without even the notion of nonexistence.

101

Indestructibility

When we consider someone to be indestructible, we generally mean that he is well established in his discipline, such as a person who has mastered the art of warfare or studied philosophy in great depth. Because such a person has mastered all sorts of techniques and training, we therefore consider him to be immovable or indestructible. In fact, from the tantric point of view, the attempt to secure oneself with gadgetry is a source of vulnerability rather than indestructibility.

In this case, we are not talking about indestructibility based on collecting information, tricks, or ideas. Instead we are referring to a basic attitude of trust in the nonexistence of our being. In the tantric notion of indestructibility, there is no ground, no basic premise, and no particular philosophy except one's own experience, which is extremely powerful and dynamic. It is a question of being rather than figuring out what to be or how to be.

102

One Stone Kills One Bird

SET ASIDE A TIME for sitting practice that is especially allocated for that practice. Don't say to yourself, "Well, I'm going to visit my girlfriend and I have to drive, so on my way to my girlfriend's I'll use driving as my meditation." That approach to mindfulness becomes too utilitarian, too pragmatic—killing two birds with one stone. "That way I meditate and I get a chance to see my girlfriend at the end, too." But something has to be given up somewhere. Some renunciation somewhere is necessary. One stone kills one bird.

103

Disciplines Are Stepping-Stones

In order to discipline the mind, it is essential to devote part of one's life to the practice of meditation. Disciplines are stepping-stones, but they are not a way of solving problems. The mind's cunning tricks are endless; therefore one should develop one's own way of freeing oneself from frivolousness. Meditation provides an immediate opportunity to bring one's neuroses to the surface, examine them, work with them, and recognize them as materials of the path rather than villains.

104

Post-Meditation Mindfulness

It has been said that you can't practice meditation without post-meditation mindfulness. Mindfulness throughout our lives when we are not doing sitting practice is also a part of the practice of meditation. One has to have some kind of self-consciousness in order to lead one's life properly, to be meditative. Often the term self-consciousness is used pejoratively, which is not fair. The basic point is to be precise and direct and without aim. Be there precisely. There is a need for mindfulness, which is the equivalent of self-consciousness, if you like—light-handed self-consciousness.

105

Transcending Karma

OUR PRESENT STATE OF MIND, our present spiritual development, or present domestic situation has been karmically determined up to this point by life situations in the past. The birth of further karma occurs through the constant reliving of the past. We reproduce the nest or ground or home, so that we can function continuously. Therefore, the practice of meditation is the only path that can work with karma as such.

Karma in this case is the psychological aspect of the continuity of impulse, emotions, and the subconscious mental processes that go on. These processes feed on themselves all the time, developing further, constantly, on and on. So unless there is a way of not feeding the subconscious mind, there is no way of preventing karmic situations. It doesn't matter whether we are dealing with good karma or bad karma. Both of those are the same kind of situations, from this point of view. Even if we are sowing seeds of good karma, we are nevertheless still encircled in a samsaric fortress. So from this point of view, meditation practice is a way of stepping out of that karmic situation altogether—transcending both good and bad.

106

A Sudden Glimpse of Compassion

In daily life we don't have to create the concept of letting go, of being free, or anything like that at all. We can just acknowledge the freedom that is already here—and just by remembering it, just by the idea of it, there is a quick glimpse. A sudden glimpse. That sudden glimpse of awareness that occurs in everyday life becomes the act of compassion.

107

Being Selfish

Caring completely for yourself is regarded as selfish, or for that matter, shellfish: carrying your own hut, your own shell, your own suit of armor with you. According to the traditional Buddhist stories of karmic cause and effect, we might reincarnate as tortoises or turtles, who carry their own homes around with them. So selfish and shellfish are synonymous. That's what we have to avoid.

108

Larger Vision

A LARGER WORLD exists, but we have never looked at it. We are too concerned with our microscopes and our magnifying glasses. We try to make things large by using magnifying glasses, but we have never looked at outer space with our naked eyes. If we looked into it, we could find it—but we don't have to use our binoculars and telescopes; we don't need them; they are false pretenses. We don't need any means to do this; we could just simply look at it, whatever it is, and enjoy it. An immensely larger vision of thinking and of celebration is taking place.

III

A Golden Buddha

One of the foundations of the approach to life in the mahayana, or the great vehicle, is the realization that completely perfect enlightenment, *samyaksambuddha,* is no longer a myth—it is real. Everybody carries in his or her heart a perfectly produced image of the Buddha, beautifully made, cast in gold. It's very real, delightfully real. That is the ground of the great vehicle: before you think big, you have to think real. That seems to be the starting point of the Lion's Roar, the proclamation of mahayana. Mahayana starts with the faith and conviction that nobody is condemned or confused.

112

The More We Give

We can afford to open ourselves and join the rest of the world with a sense of tremendous generosity, tremendous goodness, and tremendous richness. The more we give, the more we gain—although what we gain should not particularly be our reason for giving. Rather, the more we give, the more we are inspired to give constantly. And the gaining process happens naturally, automatically, always.

113

The Greatest Magic

There is a magical aspect of the world. That magic does not have to be sought, but it happens by itself. It is not as sensational as we might expect. The greatest magic of all is to be able to control and work with ego, our mind. So we could say that magic begins at home, with our own minds. If we couldn't practice magic at home, we would be at a loss. We would have no place to begin.

We might ask, "What is so magical about all this? We have been working with ego all along, throughout our Buddhist training. What is so special about this magic?" We don't see anything particularly extraordinary about it. That is true. It is quite ordinary. In fact, the ordinary aspect becomes so powerful that it *is* magic. If something is extraordinary, it is usually a mechanical invention, something sensational but feeble. But because of ordinariness, magic is possible. As far as tantra is concerned, magic is relating with the world on as ordinary a level as possible.

114

Individuality

In many cases, we try to avoid our individuality and instead emulate something else. That is a big problem. Individuality sometimes comes out of ego, like wanting to be an emperor, a king, or a millionaire. But individuality can also come from personal inspiration. It depends on the level of one's journey, on how far you have been able to shed your ego. We all have our own style and our own particular nature. We can't avoid it. The enlightened expression of yourself is in accord with your inherent nature.

115

Crazy Wisdom

USING THE WORD *crazy* from the English language to describe tantric experience is very tricky because of the various ideas we have about craziness. Being crazy is associated with the idea of being absurd, on the edge of lunacy. There is also a notion of craziness as being unconventional. And sometimes we talk about somebody being crazy about music or crazy about honey or sugar. I don't think crazy wisdom fits any of these examples. Instead, crazy wisdom is the basic norm or the basic logic of sanity. It is a transparent view that cuts through conventional norms or conventional emotionalism. It is the notion of relating properly with the world. It is knowing how much heat is needed to boil water to make a cup of tea, or how much pressure you should apply to educate your students. That level of craziness is very wise.

Such a wise person is well-versed in the ways of the world, and he or she has developed and understood basic logic. He knows how to build a campfire, how to pitch a tent, and how to brush his teeth. He knows how to handle himself in relating with the world, from the level of knowing how to make a good fire in the fireplace up to knowing the fine points of philosophy. So there is absolute knowledgeability. And then, on top of that, craziness begins to descend, as an ornament to the basic wisdom that is already there.

116

Loneliness

THE SANITY AND ENLIGHTENED energy that are created in the sitting practice of meditation are a personal experience. You may think that when somebody else wakes up, you are going to wake up as well. Then, even if you are in bad shape, you will be saved by somebody else's experience. Such cosmic hitchhiking is impossible. Everybody's in their own little vehicle, called a body, and there's no room for anybody else in that body. Sitting practice is independent, individual, and a very lonely journey. Aloneness is the basic point. When you sit, either in a group or on your own, there is a basic sense of loneliness. You feel that you're on the path and your particular path is special to you; it's extraordinary to you. It would take a long time to verbally relate such experience to somebody else.

Sometimes a student may feel completely isolated and cut off. However, he or she might also experience this loneliness as the basis of heroism in the positive sense. You are making a journey. Nobody's telling you to make this journey, but still you are making it. The only person who can help you is someone who tells you that others have made this lonely journey, and you can do so in the same way. This approach might seem very severe, very strict, but at the same time this approach is quite a happy one because there is a sense of conviction. We don't hitchhike, but we do it ourselves. That sense of celebration is very powerful and important. It is the heart of the practice of meditation.

117

Give Yourself a Break

Give yourself a break. That doesn't mean to say that you should drive to the closest bar and have lots to drink or go to a movie. Just enjoy the day, your normal existence. Allow yourself to sit in your home or take a drive into the mountains. Park your car somewhere; just sit; just be. It sounds very simplistic, but it has a lot of magic. You begin to pick up on clouds, sunshine, and weather; the mountains, your past, your chatter with your grandmother and your grandfather, your own mother, your own father. You begin to pick up on a lot of things. Just let them pass like the chatter of a brook as it hits the rocks. We have to give ourselves some time to be.

118

Three Types of Generosity

Traditionally, there are three types of generosity. The first one is ordinary generosity, giving material goods or providing comfortable situations for others. The second one is the gift of fearlessness. You reassure others and teach them that they don't have to feel completely tormented and freaked out about their existence. You help them to see that there is basic goodness and spiritual practice, that there is a way for them to sustain their lives. The third type of generosity is the gift of dharma, the teachings. You show others that there is a path that consists of discipline, meditation, and intellect or knowledge. Through all three types of generosity, you can open other people's minds. In that way their closedness, wretchedness, and small thinking can be turned into a larger vision.

119

No Enemy

For the Shambhala warrior, the actual, basic notion of victory is not so much that you have one-upped your enemy and therefore you are victorious. Rather, no enemy exists at all; therefore, there is victory. This is the idea of unconditional warriorship and unconditional victory. In connection with this, the concept of sacredness is that fearlessness is carried into everyday life situations, even brushing your teeth. So fearlessness occurs all over the place, all the time. Fearlessness here is also unconditional. In this way, fearlessness becomes cheerful and very light. There's no need for cowardice or fear at all, or any moments of doubt. Actually what we're talking about is doubtlessness, we could say, rather than fearlessness. There's no doubt. There are no second thoughts. Everything is a complete warrior's world. So here victory is not having to deal with an enemy at all. It is the notion of no enemy. The whole world is a friend.

120

Emptiness

When we talk of emptiness, it means the absence of solidity, the absence of fixed notions which cannot be changed, which have no relationship to us at all but which remain as they are, separate. The solidity of experience is a certain kind of determination not to give away, not to open. We would like to keep everything intact purely for the purpose of security, of knowing where we are. You are afraid to change. That sort of solidness is form. In the Buddha's teachings on emptiness, the statement "form is empty" refers to the absence of that security; you see everything as penetrating and open. But that doesn't mean that everything has to be completely formless, or nothing. When we talk of nothingness, emptiness, or voidness, we are not talking in terms of negatives but in terms of nothingness being everything. It's another way of saying "everything"—but it is much safer to say "nothing" at that particular level than "everything."

121

Self-Deception

Most of the problems in life do not come about because you are an aggressive or lustful person. The greatest problem is that you want to bottle those things up and put them aside, and you have become an expert in deception. That is one of the biggest problems. Meditation practice is supposed to uncover any attempts to develop a subtle, sophisticated, deceptive approach. It is to uncover those patches.

122

The Wall of Ego

IF ANYONE gets too near the wall that ego has built, the ego feels insecure; it thinks that it is being attacked and then thinks that the only way to defend itself is to ward off the threat by showing an aggressive attitude. However, when one experiences a threat—whether it is illness, undesirable characteristics, or literal opponents—the only way to develop a balanced state of being is not to try to get rid of those things, but to understand them and make use of them. Thus, the development of egolessness—the opposite of ego's game—leads one to the concept of *ahimsa* or nonviolence.

123

Realizing Nonexistence

Shunyata LITERALLY MEANS "openness" or "emptiness." Shunyata is basically understanding nonexistence. When you begin realizing nonexistence, then you can afford to be more compassionate, more giving. A problem is usually that we would like to hold on to our territory and fixate on that particular ground. Once we begin to fixate on that ground, we have no way to give. Understanding shunyata means that we begin to realize that there is no ground to get, that we are ultimately free, nonaggressive, open. We realize that we are actually nonexistent ourselves. Then we can give. We have lots to gain and nothing to lose at that point.

124

Ultimate Freedom

Freedom is the possibility of being generous. You can afford to open yourself and walk on the path easily—without defending yourself or watching yourself or being self-conscious all the time. It is the absence of ego, the absence of self-consciousness. That is ultimate freedom. The absence of self-consciousness brings generosity. You don't have to watch for dangers or be careful that you are going too fast or too slow. It is this confidence that is freedom, rather than breaking free from chains of imprisonment, exactly. Developing confidence and breaking out of psychological, internal imprisonment brings freedom naturally.

125

We Have Everything

We are noble sons and daughters of Buddha. We *are* Buddha. We have Buddha in us. Why should we crunch ourselves down and deform our state of being? Why don't we just expand ourselves into our perfect form, our perfect being? We have perceptions and energies and inspiration. We have everything. We have a spiritual friend, we have the teaching. What more do we want? We have everything in this whole universe. We can afford to extend ourselves a bit more. This approach is called the mahayana, the great vehicle, the *bodhisattva* path of those dedicated to helping others. It is heroic.

126

The Soft Spot of Compassion

Compassion is based on some sense of "soft spot" in us. It is as if we had a pimple on our body that was very sore—so sore that we do not want to rub it or scratch it. That sore spot on our body is an analogy for compassion. Why? Because even in the midst of immense aggression, insensitivity to our life, or laziness, we always have a soft spot, some point we can cultivate—or at least not bruise. Every human being has that kind of basic sore spot, including animals. Whether we are crazy, dull, aggressive, ego-tripping, whatever we might be, there is still that sore spot taking place in us. An open wound, which might be a more vivid analogy, is always there. We are not completely covered with a suit of armor all the time. We have a sore spot somewhere, some open wound somewhere. Such a relief! Thank earth!

127

Joyful Warriorship

THE TIBETAN WORD for warrior is *pawo. Pa* means "ignoring the challenger" or "ignoring the other's challenge." *Wo* makes it a noun. So the warrior is one who does not engage others' sense of aggression. When there's no aggression, trust takes place. Out of that genuine sense of warriorship comes joy. For the first time in your life, you feel at ease. "Goodness gracious! Why on earth have I been driving myself mad by being petrified by all these things around me? And how has it happened that I can finally relax?" Phew. Tremendous relaxation, which comes with a tremendous smile.

128

Celebration

HUMOR AND CELEBRATION are indivisible. Celebration means a sense of delightfulness, an uplifting quality. We could use all sorts of jargon, but fundamentally speaking, celebration is a sense of earth, actually celebrating the earth, and a sense of earth and space making love together. Humor comes from space, or sky, and earth is the celebration. When the earth begins to celebrate, space begins to make love to the earth—that's the meeting point of earth and space. Earth blossoms and sky begins to pay attention to it. Sky begins to shine all kinds of light over the earth and accommodate it with its space to grow flowers or trees, to maintain rocks, waterfalls, skyscrapers, and highways—whatever we have on this earth. We don't have to be particularly romantic about it. We're not just talking about nature, we're talking about reality.

129

Sudden Flash

In a sense, you can create a glimpse of clarity by being open to your situation—open meaning without fear of anything, complete experience. A glimpse just takes place; it takes shape on its own and sparks us. But in many cases, when a person tries to recreate a glimpse he or she had already, that sudden flash, it doesn't happen at all. The more you try, the less experience you get—you don't experience open space at all. And the minute you are just about to give up, to give in and not care—you get a sudden flash. So if you try to recapture an experience, it doesn't happen—unless you have an absence of fear and the complete confidence that these experiences don't have to be recreated, but they are there already.

130

The Fourth Moment

Nowness is sometimes referred to as the fourth moment. That may sound more mystical than what is meant. You have the past, present, and future, which are the three moments. Then you have something else taking place, which is called the fourth moment. The fourth moment is not an unusual or extraordinary experience as such. It is a state of experience that doesn't even belong to now. It doesn't belong to what might be, either. It belongs to a noncategory—which provides another sense of category. Thus it is called the fourth moment. This is the state of *vipashyana* awareness, or the state of non-ego. The Tibetan term for this means "the knowledge of egoless insight." It is a very real experience in which nothing can be misunderstood. It is such an overwhelming experience. The experience comes at you. You experience it precisely and in great detail.

131

A Constant Act of Freedom

Actual meditation practice is a constant act of freedom in the sense of being without expectation, without a particular goal, aim, and object. But as you practice meditation, as you go along with the technique, you begin to discover your present state of being. That is, we could almost say, a by-product of meditation.

132

Planning for the Future

HUMANS ARE THE ONLY ANIMALS that try to dwell in the future. You don't have to purely live in the present situation without a plan, but the future plans you make can only be based on the aspects of the future that manifest within the present situation. You can't plan a future if you don't know what the present situation is. You have to start from *now* to know how to plan.

133

A Staircase to Enlightenment

In one of the sutras, or discourses by the Buddha, he says that those who practice *shamatha* meditation, or dwelling in peace, are building a staircase toward enlightenment. To construct such a staircase to enlightenment requires precise measurement and carpentry. The boards have to be completely measured and properly built. The steps must be built properly, the angles must be looked at, and then finally we have to choose certain particular nails that can bear the pressure of people walking on them, and then we hammer them in. So when we talk about shamatha practice, the sitting practice of meditation, we are talking about building a staircase very deliberately, according to the instructions of Buddha. We might ask, "A staircase to what? What's it like at the top of the stairs?" It doesn't really matter. It's just a staircase. We are just building a staircase. No promise, no blame. Let us simplify the whole situation. Let us just build this particular staircase, very simply and directly.

134

Windhorse

THERE IS AN UPLIFTED quality that exists in our lives. You could call it sacred existence, which is automatically created because of your mindfulness and awareness. We pay attention to details: we wash the dishes, we clean our room, we press our shirts, and we fold the sheets. When we pay attention to everything around us, the overall effect is upliftedness. The Shambhalian term for that is *windhorse.* The wind principle is very airy and powerful. Horse means that the energy is rideable. That particular airy and sophisticated energy, so clean and full of decency, can be ridden. You don't just have a bird flying by itself in the sky, but you have something to ride on. Such energy is fresh and exuberant but, at the same time, rideable. Therefore, it is known as windhorse.

135

Theism and Nontheism

As far as I can see, there is no difference between theism and nontheism, basically speaking. Declaring an involvement with any kind of "-ism" turns out to be a matter of self and other. In fact, the whole question of self and other can then become very important. But if you really pursue any spiritual path, you will discover, surprisingly, that self and other are one thing. Self is other, other is self. Whether you worship someone else or you worship yourself, it is the same thing. Both theism and nontheism can be problematic if you are not involving yourself personally and fully. You may think you are becoming spiritual, but instead you could just be trying to camouflage yourself behind a religious framework—and still you will be more visible than you think.

136

Natural Hierarchy

Living in accordance with natural hierarchy is not a matter of following a series of rigid rules or structuring your days with lifeless commandments or codes of conduct. The world has order and power and richness that can teach you how to conduct your life artfully, with kindness to others and care for yourself. The discovery of natural hierarchy has to be a personal experience—magic is something you must experience for yourself. Then, you will never be tempted to put your hat on the floor, but more importantly, you will never be tempted to cheat your neighbors or your friends. You will be inspired to serve your world, to surrender yourself completely.

137

Compassion without Ground

IN ORDER to have an affectionate attitude to somebody else, you have to be without ground to begin with. Otherwise you become an egomaniac, trying to attract people out of your seduction and passion alone, or your arrogance. Compassion develops from *shunyata,* emptiness, or nonground, because you have nothing to hold on to, nothing to work with, no project, no personal gain, no ulterior motives. Therefore, whatever you do is a clean job, so to speak. So compassion and shunyata work together. It is like sunning yourself at the beach: for one thing, you have a beautiful view of the sea and the sky and everything around you, and there is also sunlight and heat and the ocean coming toward you.

138

Idiot Compassion

Idiot compassion is the highly conceptualized idea that you want to do good. Of course, according to the mahayana teachings of Buddhism you should do everything for everybody; there is no selection involved at all. But that doesn't mean to say that you have to be gentle all the time. Your gentleness should have heart, strength. In order that your compassion doesn't become idiot compassion, you have to use your intelligence. Otherwise, there could be self-indulgence, thinking that you are creating a compassionate situation when in fact you are feeding the other person's aggression. If you go to a shop and the shopkeeper cheats you and you go back and let him cheat you again, that doesn't seem to be a very healthy thing to do for others.

139

Complete Openness

THE TIBETAN WORD for generosity, *jinpa,* means giving, opening, or parting. So the notion of generosity is not holding back but giving constantly. Generosity is self-existing openness, complete openness. You are no longer subject to cultivating your own scheme or project. The best way to open yourself up is to make friends with yourself and with others.

140

Confusion

One of the main occupations of ego seems to be creating confusion. And we are willing to stick to this confusion and make it a habitual pattern of everyday life. We do this because confusion provides a tremendously stable ground to sink into. Confusion also provides a way of occupying oneself. That seems to be one of the reasons there is a continual fear of giving up or surrendering. Stepping into the open space of the meditative state of mind seems to be very irritating. Because we are quite uncertain how to handle that wakeful state, therefore we would rather run back to our own prison than be released from our prison cell. So confusion and suffering have become an occupation, often quite a secure or delightful situation.

141

Restless Mind

THIS RESTLESS MIND is buddha nature. Because it is so intelligent, therefore it is restless. It is so transparent that we can't put any patch on it to mask over the irritation—if we do, the irritation still comes through. We can't hold the irritation back or maintain ego-style comfort anymore. In tantric literature, buddha mind is referred to as a lamp in a vase. If a vase is cracked, the imperfections of the vase can be seen because of the light shining through from inside. In mahayana literature, a popular analogy refers to enlightened mind as the sun and ego's security as the clouds that prevent the sun from shining through.

The idea of buddha mind is not purely a concept or a theoretical, metaphysical idea. It is something extremely real that we can experience ourselves. In fact, it is the ego that feels that we have an ego. It is ego that tells us, "My ego is bothering me. I feel very self-conscious about having to be me. I feel that I have a tremendous burden in me, and I wonder what the best way to get rid of it is." Yet all those expressions of restlessness that keep coming out of us are the expression of buddha nature: the expression of our unborn, unobstructed, and nondwelling nature.

142

One Truth

THE ESSENCE of samsara, or confused existence, is found in the misunderstandings of bewilderment, passion, and aggression. Unless you relate to these as path—understanding them, working with them, treading on them—you do not discover the goal. So therefore, as Buddha says, "Suffering should be realized, the origin should be overcome and, by that, cessation should be realized because the path should be seen as the truth." Seeing the truth as it is, is the goal as well as the path. For that matter, discovering the truth of samsara *is* the discovery of nirvana, liberation, for truth does not depend on other formulas or alternative answers. The reality of samsara is equally the reality of nirvana. This truth is seen as one truth without relativity.

143

Implying the Truth

When you spell out the truth it loses its essence and becomes either "my" truth or "your" truth; it becomes an end in itself. When you spell out the truth, you are spending your capital while no one gets any profit. It becomes undignified, a giveaway. By implying the truth, the truth doesn't become anyone's property. When the dragon wants a rainstorm, she causes thunder and lightning. That brings the rain. Truth is generated from its environment; in that way it becomes a powerful reality. From this point of view, studying the imprint of the truth is more important than the truth itself. The truth doesn't need a handle.

144

Simplicity

SIMPLICITY is noncomplication rather than romantic simplicity. This means that there is no need for further exaggeration. Often, when we refer to somebody as simple, we mean that the person is slightly dumb or naive. He is so simple that he does not know how to be sophisticated or complicated. We might find that type of energy very refreshing, but such simplicity is regressing rather than progressing in any way. In this case, simplicity is self-existence. Something is simple because of its own magical qualities. For instance, fire burns by its own simplicity but still has its energy. A rock has its magic because it sits still and never gets bored. A river keeps flowing in a simple way; it never gets bored and never gives up its course.

145

Natural Concentration

THE ESSENCE of *bodhi,* or wakefulness, is the discovery that within the continuity of mindfulness there is a natural state of mindfulness, a natural state of being. As the discipline of the *bodhisattva,* the practitioner in the mahayana, becomes more and more perfect and she is able to concentrate fully, she realizes that she does not need to concentrate anymore; the concentration develops within her. That natural state of concentration is what is known as the insight of bodhi.

146

Change Your Attitude

THE BASIC mahayana vision is to work for the benefit of others and create a situation that will benefit others. The obstacle to becoming a mahayanist is not having enough sympathy for others and for oneself. And that problem can be dealt with by practical training, which is known as *lojong* practice, "training the mind."

One of the lojong slogans is "Change your attitude but remain natural." Generally, our attitude is that we always want to protect our own territory first. We want to preserve our own ground—others come afterward. The point of this slogan is to change that attitude around, so that we actually reflect on others first and on ourselves later. It is very simple and direct. You usually practice gentleness and tenderness toward yourself, and the opposite of that toward others. Changing your attitude means reversing your attitude altogether—instead of making someone else do something, you do it yourself.

Then the slogan says, "remain natural," which has a sense of relaxation. It means taming your basic being, taming your mind altogether so that you are not constantly pushing other people around. Instead, you take the opportunity to blame yourself. We are talking about changing your attitude of cherishing yourself. Instead of cherishing yourself, you cherish others—and then you just relax. That's it. It's very simple-minded.

147

Look!

Look. This is your world! You can't not look. There is no other world. This is your world; it is your feast. You inherited this; you inherited these eyeballs; you inherited this world of color. Look at the greatness of the whole thing. Look! Don't hesitate—look! Open your eyes. Don't blink, and look, look—look further.

Then you might *see* something. The more you look, the more inquisitive you are, the more you are bound to see. Your looking process is not restrained, because you are genuine, you are gentle, you have nothing to lose, and you have nothing to fight against. You can look so much, you can look further, and then you can see so beautifully. In fact, you can feel the warmth of red and the coolness of blue and the richness of yellow and the penetrating quality of green—all at once. You appreciate the world around you. It is a fantastic new discovery of the world.

148

Elegance

ELEGANCE MEANS appreciating things as they are. There is a sense of delight and of fearlessness. You are not fearful of dark corners. If there are any dark, mysterious corners, black and confusing, you override them with your glory, your sense of beauty, your sense of cleanness, your feeling of being regal. Because you can override fearfulness in this way, tantra, or the highest stage in Tibetan Buddhist practice, is known as the king of all the *yanas* or stages on the path. You take an attitude of having perfectly complete and very rich basic sanity.

149

Discovering Totality

Becoming more clearly aware of emotions and life situations and the space in which they occur might open us to a still more panoramic awareness. A compassionate attitude, a warmth, develops at this point. It is an attitude of fundamental acceptance of oneself while still retaining critical intelligence. We appreciate the joyful aspect of life along with the painful aspect. Relating to emotions ceases to be a big deal. Emotions are as they are, neither suppressed nor indulged but simply acknowledged. So the precise awareness of details leads into an openness to the complex totality of situations.

150

Constant Change

WE DIE SO THAT WE CAN BE REBORN. We are born so that we can die. Blossoms bloom in the spring so that there will be seeds in the autumn. Then the winter gives the seeds time to adapt to the soil. Then spring comes again. Having settled down into the ground, after their hibernation, the seeds are reawakened. Then the plants grow, and there are more seeds. Then another spring comes, another summer comes, another autumn comes, and so forth. Things change constantly, always.

151

Living on the Razor's Edge

Nowness is the sense that we are attuned to what is happening. The past is fiction and the future is a dream, and we are just living on the edge of a razor blade. It is extraordinarily sharp, extraordinarily tentative and quivering. We try to establish ground but the ground is not solid enough, because it is too sharp. We are quivering between that and this. This razor-blade quality is something more than psychological irritation. Life as a whole becomes penetratingly sharp—unavoidable and at the same time cutting. We could say that is the living description of the truth that life contains pain. According to Buddhism, life or existence is defined according to the truth of suffering, which is the razor blade.

152

Boredom and Compassion

THE BUILDINGS or the houses or the trees or the people in the world as such are not projections. What we make out of them are the projections—our version of the buildings, our version of the landscape, the people, the trees. It is the new coat of paint that we put on them. One of the biggest problems is that we are unable to develop compassion or a sympathetic attitude toward our projections, let alone toward things outside our projections—other people, other life situations. We can't even take a sympathetic attitude toward ourselves and our own projections, and that causes a lot of frustration and complications. The boredom of meditation demands your attention; in other words, the boredom becomes the sympathetic environment in relation to which you can develop compassion. In that boredom you have no choice but to relate directly to what is happening to you.

153

The Big Project

Working with the basic bewilderment or uncertainty of mind is a huge project, an enormous project. This project has been the battlefield between enlightenment and samsara, or confusion, for billions of years. And this project has become the heart of spirituality. It seems much better and more sensible to get into the big project first and try to deal with the greatest problems and difficulties that exist, rather than trying to pick up the crumbs first. We may say to ourselves, "Well, let me tidy up before we get into this big thing." You are chickening out, because you find all kinds of little things that you can tidy up, to make sure that you don't have to get to the big project, which is a very big deal from some point of view. So it seems necessary to take some kind of leap; jump into the state of heroism. We should launch the big project without discussing little details, without even asking how to do it. Whenever we talk about how to do it or what is the right way, we are talking in terms of saving ourselves from problems and pain. We are trying to buy a pair of gloves or a pair of pliers so that we don't have to strain our hands in dealing with things. Instead, we can use our naked hand to deal with our naked mind, very directly and precisely.

154

Simple-Minded

Sometimes we question our state of mind. We are concerned about the state of our sanity, the state of our mind, and we question how many preconceptions we are laying on our world or ourselves—being too heavy- or too light-handed. When all those questions are coming up, sometimes even though the motivation and the situation to work with these preoccupations might be right, and even though our understanding might be accurate, at the same time, our preoccupations begin to drive us into complete confusion. We would like to split hairs, constantly questioning the question of the question of the question of the question, constantly again and again and again. Then we don't find any room to actually allow ourselves to practice, to sit and develop any discipline at all. So there is value in the simple-mindedness of students or we could almost say their uneducatedness—not having too much vocabulary to describe their experience. At the same time, that earthbound quality provides a lot of room and space to understand the teachings to the fullest, very precisely, on a real, direct, and straightforward level.

155

Writing Your Mind

I'VE BEEN ASKED about the role that poetry could play in the journey of a Buddhist practitioner. Through poetry, you could find your own state of mind. That's precisely the concept of haiku: writing your mind. People shouldn't be too dilettantish or artistic, but they should write their own state of mind on a piece of paper. That's the meaning of the slogan "first thought best thought." We have to be very careful that we don't put too many cosmetics on our own thinking. Thoughts don't need lipstick or powder.

156

Becoming More Perceptive

THE SITTING PRACTICE of meditation allows a sense of solidness and a sense of slowness and the possibility of watching one's mind operating all the time. Out of that, a sense of expansion slowly begins to develop and, at the same time, the awareness that you have been missing a lot of things in your life. You have been too busy to look for them or see them or appreciate them. So as you begin to meditate, you become more perceptive. Your mind becomes clearer and clearer, like an immaculate microscope lens.

157

Healthy Openness

Openness doesn't necessarily mean that you have to make yourself available to another person all the time. Openness is knowing the situation—knowing if it's healthy and helpful for you to involve yourself with another person. Is showing this kind of commitment to this person healthy for him or her? Openness doesn't mean you have to take everything in at all; you have a right to reject or accept—but when you reject you don't close yourself; you reject the situation. Whether you accept or reject it depends on whether it's a healthy situation for the other person or not; it's not purely what they want. Openness doesn't mean that you are doing purely what the other person wants. Their wantingness may not be particularly accurate. So you just work along with what's valuable there.

158

Illumination

ENLIGHTENMENT is referred to as en-*lighten*-ment, rather than as a big gain of freedom. It is further luminosity: it illuminates life. Up to this point, we had a very bad lighting system; but now we are getting a better lighting system, so we begin to see every curve of skin, every inch of our world, properly. We might get very irritated by such sharpness and precision, but that seems to be part of the perspective.

159

Being Kind to Yourself

We have to learn to be kinder to ourselves, much more kind. Smile a lot, although nobody is watching you smile. Listen to your own brook, echoing yourself. You can do a good job. In the sitting practice of meditation, when you begin to be still, hundreds of thousands, millions, and billions of thoughts will go through your mind. But they just pass through, and only the worthy ones leave their fish eggs behind. We have to leave ourselves some time to be. You're not going to see the Shambhala vision, you're not even going to survive unless you leave yourself a minute to be, a minute to smile. Please give yourself a good time.

160

See the World

Sometimes, when we perceive the world, we perceive without language. We perceive spontaneously, with a pre-language system. But sometimes when we view the world, first we think a word and then we perceive. In other words, the first instance is directly feeling or perceiving the universe; the second is talking ourselves into seeing the universe. So either you look and see beyond language—as first perception—or you see the world through the filter of your thoughts, by talking to yourself. Synchronizing mind and body is looking and seeing directly beyond language. When you feel that you can afford to relax and perceive the world directly, then your vision can expand. You can see on the spot with wakefulness. Your eyes begin to open, wider and wider, and you see that the world is colorful and free and so precise.

161

Recollection

THE BUDDHIST SCRIPTURES talk about resting or abiding in recollection. The best English equivalent of this is mindfulness. "Recollection" in this case does not mean dwelling on the past but being in the present. That flow that takes place—you could be with it.

Our present state of mind is based on a reference point. Without a reference point, we can't think, we can't eat, we can't sleep, we can't behave. We have to have some reference point as to how to eat, when to stop eating, how to walk, when to stop walking, how to conduct our life—which way? This way, that way, the other way, some other way altogether? All those choices are guided by a reference point. "This is good to do; therefore I am doing this; this is not good to do, therefore I am doing that." There are choices upon choices taking place constantly. Attending to those choices and their reference points is known as recollection, *smriti* in Sanskrit. This is not exactly bringing the past to the present, but still in order to be in the present, you need memory, which is an automatic thing.

162

Mindfulness of Body

MINDFULNESS OF BODY has to do with trying to remain human, rather than becoming an animal or fly or etheric being. It means just trying to remain a human being, an ordinary human being. The basic starting point for this is solidness, groundedness. When you sit you actually sit. Even your floating thoughts begin to sit on their own bottoms.

163

Settling Down

In the Shambhala teachings, we may talk about elegance and beauty and such highfalutin stuff as kingship. But we are fundamentally talking about settling down and having a home. Maybe you should get married. Find out about taking care of a child, having a husband or wife, having a home. It will change your entire life! Go look for a mate, have a baby, have a beautiful home, whatever you can afford. You might marry a rich man or woman, but even if you don't, you can make your home beautiful. The point is that we're talking about *life.* Of course, not every Shambhalian is going to get married. The main point is not feeding one's ego or one's self-deception.

164

The Seasons of Life

THERE ARE SEASONS in your life in the same way as there are seasons in nature. There are times to cultivate and create, when you nurture your world and give birth to new ideas and ventures. There are times of flourishing and abundance, when life feels in full bloom, energized and expanding. And there are times of fruition, when things come to an end. They have reached their climax and must be harvested before they begin to fade. And finally, of course, there are times that are cold and cutting and empty, times when the spring of new beginnings seems like a distant dream. Those rhythms in life are natural events. They weave into one another as day follows night, bringing, not messages of hope and fear, but messages of how things *are.* If you realize that each phase of your life is a natural occurrence, then you need not be swayed, pushed up and down by the changes in circumstance and mood that life brings. You find that you have an opportunity to be fully in the world at all times and to show yourself as a brave and proud individual in any situation.

165

Communication

SPEECH ALONE is not the only method of communication. There is already communication before we say anything, even if we are only saying "Hello" or "How are you?" Somehow communication also continues after we finish speaking. The whole thing must be conducted in a very skillful way, by being true and not self-centered. Then the concept of duality is absent and the right pattern of communication is established. It is only through one's own experience of searching that this can be achieved, and not through merely copying someone else's example. We have to make the first move ourselves rather than expecting it to come from the phenomenal world or from other people.

166

Peace

SHAMATHA is the basic practice of Buddhist meditation. Shamatha literally means "development of peace." Peace in this case does not mean the opposite of war. Peace here has nothing to do with politics or a feeling of peacefulness that is based on artificially uplifting ourselves. The peace we are talking about in this case is non-action. It's precisely the feeling we have when we sit down to relax. When we have had a very difficult time with our friends or our parents or we have had a difficult time dealing with our business, finally we can sit down. "Phew." We're talking about that kind of flop. However, I don't want you to misunderstand, thinking that in meditation practice you can get this peace instantly. We also have to apply exertion and patience.

167

Just Be

JUST BE WITH YOUR BREATH; be with your discursive thoughts. That purity brings a sense of relief and a sense of peace, which is known as individual salvation. Peace in this case means being without complications. It is not a state of tranquility per se; it is just basic simplicity and basic ordinariness. That peace, that simplicity, is empty by nature. It has nothing to dwell on or with; therefore, it is basically fresh and clean and free from dirt, free from sloppiness. It is empty.

168

Regularity Is Not the Point

The truth about you has different facets, obviously. You might think you are made out of some good things and some bad things. Sometimes you feel bad and sometimes good. Life may be monotonous, but there are ups and downs as well. Regularity in life is not the point; experience is the point.

169

A Subtle Twist of Mind

LITTLE THINGS CAUSE a shift in our attention, no matter how small or little they might be. But in the end, things tend to get exaggerated immensely. So suffering comes from such little twists that take place in our life. That first little hint of dislike for somebody or that first hint of attraction for somebody eventually escalates and could bring on a much more immense scale of emotional drama or psychodrama. Everything starts from a minute scale at the beginning and then expands. It begins to swell, so to speak, and expand in that way until it becomes very large—immeasurably large in a lot of cases. We experience ourselves that way. Within that frame of reference, that subtle shift of attention seems to be the important cause of suffering in our life. Such shifts of attention make emotions as they are: aggression, passion, ignorance, and all the rest of them. They are seemingly very heavy-handed and large-scale and crude. But they have their origin in a subtle twist that takes place in our mind constantly, all the time.

170

Drop All Reference Points

WE MUST DROP all reference points, all concepts of what is or what should be. Then it is possible to experience the uniqueness and vividness of phenomena directly. There is tremendous room to experience things, to allow experience to occur and pass away. Movement happens within vast space. Whatever happens, pleasure and pain, birth and death, and so forth, are not interfered with but are experienced in their fullest flavor. Whether they are sweet or sour, they are experienced completely, without philosophical overlays or emotional attitudes to make things seem lovable or presentable. We are never trapped in life, because there are constant opportunities for creativity, challenges for improvisation. Ironically, by seeing clearly and acknowledging our egolessness, we may discover that suffering contains bliss, impermanence contains continuity or eternity, and egolessness contains the earth quality of solid being. But this transcendental bliss, continuity, and beingness are not based on fantasies, ideas, or fears.

171

The Victorious One

ANY PRINCIPLE of holding onto your ego is the complete opposite of the Buddhist tradition. But on the other hand, when you develop full awareness, like the Buddha, you become a king automatically. The epithet or title for the Buddha is *vijaya,* from the word *jayanti,* meaning "the victorious one," which is the equivalent of kinghood. Basically speaking, being capable of extending love and affection to yourself is the starting point.

172

Fear and Fearlessness

Cowardice, or uncertainty, comes from speed, from not being on the spot, and from not being able to lead life properly and fully. You miss a lot of details, and you also miss the overview. To correct that, you need room for fearlessness, which comes from having faith in your existence. Basically speaking, fearlessness is not particularly a reward or a goal, but fearlessness is part of the journey on the path. Fearlessness alternates with fear, and both of those are kindling for the fire. You are nervous, speedy, fearful. Then that brings another area of steadiness, solidity, and calm. So fear and fearlessness constantly alternate.

173

Truth Is Like a Thunderbolt

DHARMA literally means "truth" or "norm." It is a particular way of thinking, a way of viewing the world, which is not a concept but experience. This particular truth is very painful truth—usually truths are. It rings with the sound of reality, which comes too close to home. We become completely embarrassed when we begin to hear the truth. It is wrong to think that the truth is going to sound fantastic and beautiful, like a flute solo. The truth is actually like a thunderbolt. It wakes you up and makes you think twice whether you should stay in the rain or move into the house. Provocative.

174

The Great Joy

MEDITATION PRACTICE is based on dropping dualistic fixation, dropping the struggle of good against bad. There are many references in the tantric literature to *mahasukha,* the great joy, but the reason it is referred to as the great joy is because it transcends both hope and fear, pain and pleasure. Joy here is not pleasurable in the ordinary sense, but it is an ultimate and fundamental sense of freedom, a sense of humor, the ability to see the ironical aspect of the game of ego, the play of polarities. If one is able to see ego from an aerial point of view, then one is able to see its humorous quality.

175

The Mouse and the Turquoise

THERE IS THE Tibetan story of a certain monk who renounced his samsaric, confused life and decided to go live in a cave in order to meditate all the time. Prior to this he had been thinking continually of pain and suffering. His name was Ngonagpa of Langru, the black-faced one of Langru, because he never smiled at all but saw everything in life in terms of pain. He remained in retreat for many years, very solemn and deadly honest, until one day he looked at the shrine and saw that someone had presented a big lump of turquoise as a gift to him. As he viewed the gift, he saw a mouse creep in and try to drag away the piece of turquoise. The mouse could not do it, so it went back to its hole and called another mouse. They both tried to drag away this big lump of turquoise but could not do it. So they squeaked together and called eight more mice that came and finally managed to drag the whole lump back into their hole. Then for the first time Ngonagpa of Langru began to laugh and smile. And that was his first introduction to openness, a sudden flash of enlightenment.

176

The Truth of Insecurity

FUNDAMENTALLY, every one of us feels extremely insecure. You could have lots of money, lots of background, education, friends, resources, skills, but none of that is going to make any difference to your security. The more we seek security, the more insecurity that creates. It constantly happens that way. There's something fundamentally threatening and insecure taking place all the time in our lives. Something's not quite as solid as we would like it to be, so we need lots of reassurance—some philosophy, some idea, some kind of backing from the world of comfort, the world of companionship. There is always hollowness, an emptiness taking place in us always. Basically, we feel we are broke and we have a poverty mentality. Very few people like to face that, but it's the first truth, one of the very valuable truths to face. It is not really pleasant, and it may not even seem helpful, for that matter. But maybe its unhelpfulness is helpful. There's always that possibility.

177

No Time Off

A WARRIOR never needs to take time off. Trying to relax by slouching or indulging in habitual patterns only produces schizophrenia. You are such a nice person at the office, but the minute you come home you turn on the television, argue with your spouse, and send your children to their rooms, telling them you need peace and quiet. Such habitual patterns are dangerous and destructive. They prevent you from seeing the Great Eastern Sun, the experience of human wakefulness. Uplifting your head and shoulders may sometimes give you back pain or a strained neck, but uplifting yourself is necessary. The journey may be demanding, but there is no way of avoiding it.

178

The Inexhaustible Energy of Emotions

In the practice of meditation, we neither encourage emotions nor repress them. By seeing them clearly, by allowing them to be as they are, we no longer permit them to serve as a means of entertaining and distracting us. Thus, they become the inexhaustible energy that fulfills egoless action.

179

Conversing with Our Negativity

You can always count on the fact that our aspect of viciousness or apelike quality will reflect back to us. Then we can either project it onto somebody else or we can reflect and realize the situation within ourselves. Quite precisely, when you are in that particular state of mind, there is a kind of conversation going on. You may try to tell yourself to calm down and not worry. But then the undercurrent of the force of the projection tries to pierce through again and again. There is always this conversation going on with one's own negativity. The neurotic aspect of mind is always willing to fall into either the extreme of left or right. The right extreme is anger, the masculine extreme. The left is passion, the feminine extreme. This symbolism is true and universal—a cosmic symbol, which happens with all of life. These symbols are not based on Indian, Buddhist, or Tibetan stories at all. These are utterly cosmic principles, as far as the symbolism is concerned.

180

Seeing the Transparency of Concepts

In the absence of thoughts and emotions, the lords, or the forces, of materialism bring up a still more powerful weapon, concepts. Labeling phenomena creates a feeling of a solid, definite world of "things." Such a solid world reassures us that we are a solid, continuous thing as well. The world exists, therefore I, the perceiver of the world, exist. Meditation involves seeing the transparency of concepts, so that labeling no longer serves as a way of solidifying our world and our image of self. Labeling becomes simply the act of discrimination.

181

Purification

PURIFICATION is learning to relate with problems. Does a problem exist or not? Is the problem a problem, or is the problem a promise? We are not talking about how to get rid of problems or impurities here, as though we were suddenly surrounded by piles of garbage that we want to clean up. That is not the point. The point is to discover the quality of garbageness. Before we dispose of our garbage, first we have to examine it. If we approached purification as simply trying to get rid of our garbage, we would do a great job of emitting spiritual pollution into the atmosphere.

182

In or Out?

Ideas are not solid, if they are not founded on aggression or dogma. We can have open ideas. There is no problem with that. Ideas are not really founded on solid ground at all. They are just . . . ideas, which is a very important point. If you completely buy into someone else's idea or version of spirituality, it's like being caught in the jaws of a crocodile. This is one of the problems with many approaches to spirituality: either you are in it or you are not in it. In or out. You can't actually experience the space between the two. That is a problem, and that seems to be a spiritual materialistic trick to use on people: trying to save them from their experience. That approach is based on a hesitation or inability to provide everything legitimately, step by step. If the leaders of a spiritual group feel somewhat inadequate, they may tell potential students, "Buy it or don't buy it." That seems to be too cheap. Spiritual discipline is not based on becoming somebody else. But you become you in your enlightened version. That is the whole point.

183

A Gap in Time

HUNDREDS OF YEARS AGO, students practiced meditation in caves. There's not very much difference between the experience of a practitioner then and our experience now. The main difference is that they heard different noises then. These days we might hear airplanes flying above, and in those days, they might have heard flies buzzing about. In actual reality, as far as the living situation is concerned, it's essentially the same, then and now.

In those days, caves were routinely used for sitting practice, not for romantic reasons but because, in that geographical area, there were lots of caves. You didn't have to spend money to build a cabin; there were holes in the mountains already. You just went and lived there. Nowadays, we can't find many holes in the mountains around here, so we have to build retreat cabins. It's simply a question of geography.

Actually things haven't changed that much. We might romanticize the "good old days," but if you were there right now, you wouldn't think that those were the "good old days" at all. You would have the same experience then as now, anyway. It's just a gap in time, a time lapse.

184

Steady Mind

THE SANSKRIT WORD for meditation is *dhyana;* the Tibetan term is *samten.* Both refer to the same thing: steady mind. Mind is steady in the sense that you don't go up when a thought goes up, and you don't go down when it goes down, but you just watch things going either up or down. Whether good or bad, exciting, miserable, or blissful thoughts arise—whatever occurs in your state of mind, you don't support it by having an extra commentator.

The sitting practice of meditation is simple, direct, and very businesslike. You just sit and watch your thoughts go up and down. There is a physical technique in the background, which is working with the breath as it goes out and in. That provides an occupation during sitting practice. It is partly designed to occupy you so that you don't evaluate thoughts. You just let them happen.

In that environment, you can develop renunciation: you renounce extreme reactions to your thoughts. Warriors on the battlefield don't react to success or failure. Success or failure is just regarded as another breath coming in and going out, another discursive thought coming in and going out. So the warrior is very steady. Because of that, the warrior is victorious—because victory is not particularly the aim or the goal. But the warrior can just be—as he or she is.

185

The Golden Key

IF YOU ARE LOST in the desert, without food and water, even if you have lots of gold in your pack, you can't eat it and you can't drink it—so you are still starved and parched. That is analogous to what happens to many people who have money. They have no idea how to eat it and how to drink it. People can spend thousands of dollars and still be dissatisfied and in tremendous pain. Even with all that supposed wealth, they may still be unable to enjoy a simple meal. True wealth does not come about automatically. It has to be cultivated; you have to earn it. Otherwise, even if you have lots of money, you will still be starved. So if you want to rule your world, please don't think that means you have to spend a great deal of money. The key to wealth, or the golden key, is appreciating that you can be poor—or I should say, unmoneyed—and still feel good, because you have a sense of wealthiness in any case, already. That is the wonderful key to richness and the first step in ruling: appreciating that wealth and richness come from being a basically decent human being. You do not have to be jealous of those who have more, in an economic sense, than you do. You can be rich even if you are poor.

186

Heaven

DHARMA ART has to do with the state of mind of the artist and how we can communicate that fully to ourselves and to our world. In this regard, heaven is space. It provides psychological space in your state of mind, the sense that there's enough room for you to work. The space of heaven is primordial mind, free from constrictions. It is not blank or vacant, but it accommodates everything. It has the quality of wakefulness, the quality of delight, and the quality of brilliance. So the general meaning of heaven is some kind of totality in which we can operate. We can actually walk, dance, kick, and stretch ourselves in that atmosphere. There's lots of room, lots of freedom, and also a sense of wakefulness. That kind of space becomes an integral part of the process of creation.

187

Advice to Businesspeople

CONDUCTING BUSINESS and brushing our teeth should be regarded as the same kind of situation. Our business philosophy should be based on meditation practice, an understanding of the dharma, the teachings, and some kind of genuineness. You should have a settled attitude, even if your business is only six months old. First of all, you should know who you are. From that, you can know how you are going to manifest yourself.

You might talk to other businesspeople, who say, "Great, just go ahead! Let me jump in with you." Those little enthusiasms sound suspicious. In fact, many businesses have suffered in the past by trying to snowball each other's enthusiasm to the level of frivolity. We should be aware that once we begin to do that, we are trying to catch an echo in a net. We begin to run here and there looking for the origin of the echo, but our net will always be empty. Nothing is caught, because there is nothing in it.

On the whole, there is no particular trick to conducting a successful business. Even if the Buddha himself or Padmasambhava, the father of Buddhism in Tibet, set up a business, there would be no trick. We have to go along with the natural sense of economy that exists in this country, and with basic sanity.

188

The Absence of Struggle Is Freedom

By the examination of his own thoughts, emotions, concepts, and the other activities of mind, the Buddha discovered that there is no need to struggle to prove our existence, that we need not be subject to the rule of the lords or forces of materialism. There is no need to struggle to be free; the absence of struggle is in itself freedom. This egoless state is the attainment of buddhahood. The process of transforming the material of mind from expressions of ego's ambition into expressions of basic sanity and enlightenment through the practice of meditation—this might be said to be the true spiritual path.

189

The Magic of Individuality

Perceptions are not governed by one statement alone, but by individuals reacting to the basic elements. When individuals react to air, water, fire, space, or earth, they have different responses. Individually, they have different perspectives on all that. Those differences do not become uniform at all—they are ongoing. The magic lives in that individuality. We are relating individually to all kinds of basic things in life that we seemingly share. But we have no idea, exactly, if this is true. None of us has had a chance to tell each other precisely what our perception of water is like. We could use all kinds of words and ideas and concepts and terms, but that still would not make it clear. That would be somebody else's concepts. There is a basic iconographic pattern in the universe, like the existence of the seasons and the elements, but how we react to that is individual.

190

Self-Existing Energy

SELF-EXISTING ENERGY takes place continuously. Although the source of such energy is difficult to track down, it is universal and all-pervasive. It happens by itself, naturally. It is based on enthusiasm as well as freedom: enthusiasm in the sense that we trust what we are doing, and freedom in the sense that we are completely certain that we are not going to be imprisoned by our own energy, but instead, freed constantly.

According to the tantric tradition of nontheism, energy is vital and important. From that point of view, working with energy, or developing *siddhi,* means that we relate directly to our domestic world, our enemies, our friends, our relatives, business partners, policemen, the government, or whatever happens in our life. We relate directly with energy as much as possible.

We are not talking about centralizing energy within ourselves. Working with energy in a tantric sense is a decentralized process. We are talking about energy as all and everywhere. In Buddhist tantra, energy is openness and all-pervasiveness. It is constantly expanding. It is decentralized energy, a sense of flood, ocean, outer space, the light of the sun and moon.

191

Art on the Spot

AN ARTIST PRODUCES A WORK of art on the spot. Each instant, there are on-the-spot moments of sanity, connected with the healthiness of the artist's state of mind and his or her relationship to the medium and the work of art itself. According to the Buddhist tradition, neurosis refers to that state of mind which fixates and holds onto things. It is broken down into three categories: passion, which is too gooey, too much glue; aggression, which is too sharp, too threatening, too rejecting; and ignorance, which is a state of stupor that cannot discriminate left from right or black from white. Basically, we're talking about the absence of that in the creation of a work of art, the absence of neurotic mind.

192

Grasping

When we don't cling to things, because we don't have to have them, we can develop a basic understanding of things as they are. We can let go of the reference point of grasping onto things: the sights, sounds, smells, tastes, and other reference points we usually feel we need. We don't need to draw companionship of any kind from such things. We do not need to depend on such reference points. We do not need to closet ourselves in with personal reference points in order to clutch onto the hot breath of our particular dear old life that breathes so heavily on us.

193

Real Humility

HUMILITY, very simply, is the absence of arrogance. Where there is no arrogance, you relate with your world as an eye-level situation, without one-upmanship. Because of that, there can be a genuine interchange. Nobody is using their message to put anybody else down, and nobody has to come down or up to the other person's level. Everything is eye-level. Humility in the Shambhala tradition also involves some kind of playfulness, which is a sense of humor. In most religious traditions, you feel humble because of a fear of punishment, pain, and sin. In the Shambhala world you feel full of it. You feel healthy and good. In fact, you feel proud. Therefore, you feel humility. That's one of the Shambhala contradictions or, we could say, dichotomies. Real humility is genuineness.

194

Crying and Laughing

As WARRIORS of Shambhala, we find ourselves shedding tears at the same time that we are smiling. We are crying and laughing at once. That is the ideal Shambhalian mentality: we cry and we smile at the same time. Isn't it wonderful? A flower needs sunshine together with raindrops to blossom so beautifully. For that matter, a rainbow is made out of the tears falling from our eyes, mixed with a shot of sunshine. That is how a rainbow becomes a rainbow—sunshine mixed with tears. From that point of view, the Shambhala philosophy is the philosophy of a rainbow.

195

Relaxation

MINDFULNESS is sometimes referred to as restful, often as relaxation. But in this case we are not talking about the sense of relaxation before you get hypnotized. We are not particularly talking about the ideal, conventional concept of relaxation, such as the relaxation you get after your yoga class, how good you feel after intensive hatha yoga postures. Here relaxation is being without defense mechanisms, or if defense mechanisms arise, letting them be. Let them defend themselves rather than defend you. Then the defense mechanisms fall apart by themselves. If you are tense, for instance, let the tenseness be tense. Then tenseness has no substance; it becomes relaxation.

196

The Warrior Is Not Afraid of Space

THE COWARD LIVES in constant terror of space: afraid of darkness because he can't see anything, afraid of silence because he can't hear anything. The setting-sun world teaches you to wear a suit of armor to protect yourself. But what are you protecting yourself from? Space. The challenge of warriorship is to step out of the cocoon, to step out into space, by being brave and at the same time gentle.

197

That One Word No

THE BASIC *no* is accepting discipline in our life without preconceptions. Normally, when we say the word "discipline," it comes with a lot of mixed feelings. It's like saying "porridge." Some people like porridge, and some people hate it. Nevertheless, porridge remains porridge. It is a very straightforward thing. We have similar feelings about discipline and the meaning of *no*. Sometimes, it's a bad *no*: it is providing oppressive boundaries that we don't want to accept. Or it could be a good *no*, which encourages us to do something healthy. But when we just hear that one word, *no*, the message is mixed.

When you were growing up, at a very early stage—perhaps around two years old—you must have heard your father or mother saying *no* to you. They would say, "No, don't get into that," or "No, don't explore that too much," or "No, be quiet. Be still." When you heard the word *no*, you may have responded by trying to fulfill that *no*, by being good. Or you may have reacted negatively, by defying your parents and their *no*, by exploring further and being "bad." That mixture of the temptation to be naughty and the desire to be disciplined occurs very early in life. When our parents say no to us, it makes us feel strange about ourselves, which becomes an expression of fear. On the other hand, there is another kind of *No*, which is very positive. We have never heard that basic *No* properly: *No* free from fear and free from doubt.

198

Reconnecting with Reality

The appreciation of simplicity has almost been lost. From London to Tokyo, there are problems with trying to create pleasure and comfort out of speed. The world is mechanized to such an extent that you don't even have to think. You just push a button and a computer gives you the answer. You don't have to learn to count. You press a button, and a machine counts for you. Casualness has become increasingly popular, because people think in terms of efficiency rather than appreciation. Why bother to wear a tie, if the purpose of wearing clothes is just to cover your body? If the reason for eating food is only to fill your stomach and provide nutrition, why bother to look for the best meat, the best butter, the best vegetables? But the reality of the world is something more than the modern world has embraced. Pleasure has been cheapened, joy has been reduced, happiness has been computerized. The goal of warriorship is to reconnect with the nowness of reality, so that you can go forward without destroying simplicity, without destroying your connection to this earth.

199

How the Warrior Meets the World

THE CONFIDENT WARRIOR conducts himself with gentleness, fearlessness, and intelligence. Gentleness is the warm quality of the human heart. Because of the warmth of his heart, the warrior's confidence is not too hard or brittle. Rather, it has a vulnerable, open, and soft quality. It is our gentleness which allows us to feel warmth and kindness and to fall in love. But at the same time we are not completely tender. We are tough as well as soft. We are fearless as well as gentle. The warrior meets the world with a slight sense of detachment, a sense of distance and precision. This aspect of confidence is the natural instinct of fearlessness which allows the warrior to meet challenges without losing his or her integrity.

200

Bravery Invokes Magic

THE BEST AND ONLY WAY to invoke *drala,* or magic, is by creating an atmosphere of bravery. The fundamental aspect of bravery is *being without deception.* Deception in this case is self-deception, doubting yourself. Usually if we say someone is brave, we mean that he is not afraid of any enemy or he is willing to die for a cause or he is never intimidated. The Shambhala understanding of bravery is quite different. Here bravery is the courage to be—to live in the world without any deception and with tremendous kindness and caring for others. You might wonder how this can bring magic into your life. The ordinary idea of magic is that you can conquer the elements, so that you can turn earth into fire or fire into water or ignore the law of gravity and fly. But true magic is the magic of *reality,* as it is: the earth of earth, the water of water—communicating with the elements so that, in some sense, they become one with you. When you develop bravery, you make a connection with the elemental quality of existence. Bravery begins to heighten your existence, that is, to bring out the brilliant and genuine qualities of your environment and of your being.

201

You Cannot Start from Perfection

In the practice of meditation, you cannot start from absolute, complete perfection. Being perfect does not matter. Just perceive and experience and disown. It does not matter how and what. The problem is that we always want to start something and at the same time make sure that what we are doing is right. But somehow we just cannot have that kind of insurance. One really has to take a chance and accept the raw and rugged quality of the situation.

You could have a commentary-type situation going on in your mind, where there is constant analysis involved. But that analysis is just part of the process. Just leave it that way. It does not have to become final. There is nothing the matter with your commentary as long as you do not try to take it as a final conclusion. It is just chatter. Let it be that way. You should not interfere with that energy that is going through. You also should not try to make it into a definite, recorded message with the idea of playing it back when you need it. Because when you play it back, you will be in a different situation so that it will automatically be out of date.

202

Work with the First Glimpse of Suffering

How can we relate with suffering without dwelling on it? Work with the first glimpse, and then boycott whatever happens afterward. We have a first impulse or first insight usually, and then after that we begin to manipulate it and make it into our own ideal concept of some kind or another. So the idea here is to just look at the first flash of pain, which is very fresh and clear, and not to comment on it anymore. Often the contemplative writings of the Buddhist tradition talk about disowning your experiences. That's a very popular term. Even if you have a semi-significant experience, still disown it, don't try to keep it. Disownership plays a very important part.

203

Let Things Take Their Course

In the practice of meditation, when bodily pain or pleasure arises, just perceive it and just leave it. You do not have to put it through any process of any kind. Each situation is unique. Therefore you just go along with it, let it happen according to its nature. It is a matter of acceptance. Even though the acceptance of what is happening may be confusing, just accept the given situation and do not try to make it something else; do not try to make it into an educational process at all. Just see it, perceive it, and then abandon it.

If you experience something and then disown that experience, you provide a space between that knowledge and yourself, which permits it simply to take its course. Disowning is like the yeast in the fermentation process. That process brews a state of mind in which you begin to learn and feel properly.

204

Wakeful Inquisitiveness

Confidence expresses itself as innate intelligence, which raises ordinary gentleness and fearlessness to the level of warriorship. In other words, it is intelligence that prevents gentleness from becoming cheap romanticism without any vision, and fearlessness from becoming purely macho. Intelligence is our sense of wakeful inquisitiveness toward the world. It is what allows us to appreciate and take delight in the vivid qualities of the world around us.

205

No Original Sin

Coming from a tradition that stresses human goodness, it was something of a shock for me to encounter the Western tradition of original sin. It seems that this notion of original sin does not just pervade Western religious ideas; it actually seems to run throughout Western thought as well, especially psychological thought. Among patients, theoreticians, and therapists alike, there seems to be great concern with the idea of some original mistake which causes later suffering—a kind of punishment for that mistake. One finds that a sense of guilt or being wounded is quite pervasive. Whether or not such people actually believe in the idea of original sin, or in God for that matter, they seem to feel that they have done something wrong in the past and are now being punished for it. The problem with this notion of original sin or mistake is that it acts very much as a hindrance to people. At some point, of course it is necessary to realize one's shortcomings. But if one goes too far with that, it kills any inspiration and can destroy one's vision as well. So in that way, it really is not helpful, and in fact it seems unnecessary. In Buddhism we do not have any comparable ideas of sin and guilt. Obviously there is the idea that one should avoid mistakes. But there is not anything comparable to the heaviness and inescapability of original sin.

206

The Compassion of the Buddha

THE BUDDHA'S DEMONSTRATIONS of basic sanity were spontaneous. He did not preach or teach in the ordinary sense but, as he unfolded, the energy of compassion and the endless resources of generosity developed within him and people began to find this out. That kind of activity of the Buddha is the *vipashyana* or awareness practice that we are attempting. It is realizing that space contains matter, that matter makes no demands on space, and that space makes no demands on matter. It is a reciprocal and open situation. Everything is based on compassion and openness. Compassion is not particularly emotional in the sense that you feel bad that someone is suffering, that you are better than others, and that you have to help them. Compassion is that total openness in which the Buddha had no ground, no sense of territory—so much so that he was hardly an individual. He was just a grain of sand living in the vast desert. Through his insignificance, he became the "world enlightened one," because there was no battle involved. The dharma he taught was passionless, without aggression.

207

The Inheret Healthiness of Your Mind

ACCORDING TO THE BUDDHIST perspective, there are problems, but they are temporary and superficial defilements that cover over one's basic goodness, or *tathagatagarbha.* This viewpoint is a positive and optimistic one. But again we should emphasize that this viewpoint is not purely conceptual. It is rooted in the experience of meditation and in the healthiness it encourages. There are temporary habitual neurotic patterns that develop based on past experience, but these can be seen through. It is just this that is studied in the *abhidharma* (the early compilations of Buddhist teachings on philosophy and psychology): how one thing succeeds another, how volitional action originates and perpetuates itself, how things snowball. And most important, abhidharma studies how, through meditation practice, this process can be cut through. Through practice, which is confirmed by study, the inherent healthiness of your mind and others' minds is experienced over and over. You see that your problems are not all that deeply rooted. You see that you can make literal progress. You find yourself becoming more mindful and more aware, developing a greater sense of healthiness and clarity as you go on, and this is tremendously encouraging.

208

Obstacles

As WARRIORS, we try to rejoice whenever there is an obstacle, and we try to regard that as something that makes us smile. Each particular setback creates a further smile. We keep on going in that way, and we never give up or give in to any obstacles. For instance, I myself had a lot of hard times getting out of my country and being ill. And all sorts of things still happen to me personally. Although everybody is trying to be extremely helpful to me, nonetheless obstacles happen to me all the time. But I don't regard those obstacles as a sign of anything at all; I keep on going, myself. I was terribly sick yesterday, and it was not very pleasant—however, it made me smile. So I'm here, smiling, right now. We will always have ups and downs. It is like riding on a roller coaster: the more you go down and the more you go up, the more you smile each time.

209

Hope versus Faith

THE EXPERIENCE of our day-to-day living situation consists of dissatisfaction, questioning, pain, depression, aggression, passion. All these are real, and we have to relate with them. Having a relationship with this may be extremely difficult. It's an organic operation without any anesthetics. If we really want to get into it, we should be completely prepared to take a chance and get nothing back but tremendous disappointment, tremendous hopelessness.

Hope is the source of pain, and hope operates on the level of something other than what there is. We hope, dwelling in the future, that things might turn out right. We do not experience the present, do not face the pain or neurosis as it is. So the only way that is feasible is developing an attitude of hopelessness, something other than future orientation. The present is worth looking at.

Faith is a more realistic attitude than hope is. Hope is a sense of lacking something in the present situation. We are hopeful about getting better as we go along. Faith is that it's okay in the present situation, and we have some sense of trust in that.

210

The Nonviolent Approach

To develop ahimsa, or the nonviolent approach, first of all you have to see that your problems are not really trying to destroy you. Usually, we immediately try to get rid of our problems. We think that there are forces operating against us and that we have to get rid of them. The important thing is to learn to be friendly toward our problems, by developing what is called *metta* in Pali, *maitri* in Sanskrit, or loving-kindness in English.

211

All-Victorious, You Have Nothing to Conquer

Being all-victorious is not a matter of talking yourself into believing that everything is okay. Rather, if you actually look, if you take your whole being apart and examine it, you find that you are genuine and good as you are. In fact, the whole of existence is well-constructed, so that there is very little room for mishaps. There are, of course, constant challenges. But for the true warrior, there is no warfare. You are never at war with your world.

212
Wholesome Learning

TEACHERS often think that if children do not feel guilty, then they won't study properly and consequently won't develop as they should. Therefore, many teachers feel that they have to do something to push the child, and guilt seems to be one of the chief techniques they use. This occurs even on the level of improving reading and writing. The teacher looks for errors: "Look, you made a mistake. What are you going to do about it?" From the child's point of view, learning is then based on trying not to make mistakes, on trying to prove you actually are not bad. It is entirely different when you approach the child more positively: "Look how much you have improved; therefore we can go further." In the latter case, learning becomes an expression of one's wholesomeness and innate intelligence.

213

Beyond Dualism

THE PHENOMENAL WORLD that all human beings experience is fickle and flexible and also merciless. You often wonder whether you can ride on that fickle and merciless situation or whether it is going to ride on you. To use an analogy, either you are riding on a donkey or the donkey is riding on you. Ordinarily, in your experience of the world, it is questionable who is riding on whom. The more you struggle to gain the upper hand, the more speed and aggression you manufacture to overcome your obstacles, the more you become subject to the phenomenal world. The real challenge is to transcend that duality altogether. It is possible to contact energy that is beyond dualism, beyond aggression—energy that is neither for you nor against you.

214
Problems as Opportunities

The attitude that results from the Buddhist orientation and practice is quite different from the "mistake mentality." One actually experiences mind as fundamentally pure, that is, healthy and positive, and "problems" as temporary and superficial defilements. Such a viewpoint does not quite mean getting rid of problems, but rather shifting one's focus. Problems are seen in a much broader context of health: one begins to let go of clinging to one's neuroses and to step beyond obsession and identification with them. The emphasis is no longer on the problems themselves but rather on the ground of experience through realizing the nature of mind itself. When problems are seen in this way, then there is less panic and everything seems more workable. When problems arise, instead of being seen as purely threats, they become learning situations, opportunities to find out more about one's own mind, and to continue on one's journey.

215

Art and Meditation

Nobody can create a perfect work of art or understand a perfect work of art without understanding the practice of meditation. So the sitting practice of meditation is the basic ground. But what do we mean by the sitting practice of meditation? For instance, Beethoven, El Greco, or my most favorite person in music, Mozart—I think they all sat. They sat in the sense that their minds became blank before they created a work of art. Otherwise, they couldn't possibly do it. Just coming out of the market and plopping down at the dining room table and writing a play—that's impossible. Some kind of mindlessness in the Buddhist sense has to take place. From that basic ground, the sense of being, openness, or isness begins to develop.

216

Conquering Fear Is Not Blocking Sensitivity

CONQUERING FEAR is not based on blocking your sensitivity. Otherwise, you become a deaf and dumb monarch, a jellyfish king. Sitting on a horse requires balance, and as you acquire that balance in the saddle, you have more awareness of the horse. So when you sit in the saddle on your fickle horse, you feel completely exposed and gentle. If you feel aggressive, you don't have a good seat. In fact, you are probably not even riding the horse. You don't put your saddle on a fence railing. You have to saddle a real horse. In this case, riding the horse is riding somebody else's mind. It requires a complete connection. In the Buddhist tradition, this is called compassion, or working with somebody else. You are completely exposed in this situation. Otherwise, it's like a medieval knight encased in his armor. It's so heavy that he has to be cranked up onto the horse. Then he rides off to battle and usually falls off. There's something wrong with that technology.

217

Exertion

EXERTION MEANS BEING CONSISTENT, committed, and faithful to the practice of meditation. Exertion is more than having a sense of duty. There is a sense that the practice of dharma is getting into your blood. That is what is known as being one with the dharma, or being a part of the dharma.

This kind of exertion doesn't come very easily. One has to be joyful, and one also has to work. There has to be a sense of taking joy in problems. This is not particularly the perverted view of taking joy in pain. The approach shouldn't be masochistic, but one has to find some joy in the obstacles. If your journey is already very arduous and difficult, and then suddenly your car has a flat tire when you are trying to get to an important place on time, you have to learn to smile. You don't leave the car there. Instead, you fix it and try to keep going.

Altogether, we have a sense of never losing heart—and never looking for alternatives, unless our situation is really, absolutely, fundamentally, totally, utterly unworkable. Otherwise, we wouldn't give in or give up. We can't expect an easy journey, an easy situation, or easy circumstances.

218

The Dragon

INSCRUTABILITY is represented by the dragon. The dragon is energetic, powerful, and unwavering. According to tradition, the dragon abides in the sky in the summer, and hibernates in the ground during the winter. When the spring comes, the dragon rises from the ground with the mist and the dew. When a storm is necessary, the dragon breathes out lightning and roars out thunder. This analogy gives us some feeling of predictability within the context of unpredictability. Inscrutability is also the state of settling down in your confidence—remaining solid and relaxed at once. You are open and fearless, free from longing and doubt, but at the same time, you are very interested in the movements of the world. Your wakefulness and intelligence make you self-contained and confident with a confidence that needs no reaffirmation through feedback. So the state of inscrutability is conviction that doesn't need confirmation. You feel a sense of genuineness, that you are not deceiving yourself or others. That notion comes from being settled.

219

Be Sensitive to Environment

ENVIRONMENT is extremely important, not only in how you treat your children but in how you treat yourself. It includes both animate and inanimate situations: your physical living situation as well as the people around you—your parents, teachers, students, maids, tutors, or whatever. Environment includes your relationship with your business partners, your cab driver, your waitress, whomever you meet. To be sane and to provide a ground of sanity for others, you need to be sensitive to environment. If you create an unbalanced or aggressive environment, it will produce a sense of separation between you and others—you and your world. Then you tend to blame everything on somebody else, which in turn brings blame onto yourself as well, at the same time.

220

Tell the Truth

Truth always works. There always has to be basic honesty; that is the source of trust. When someone sees that you are telling the truth, then they will realize further that you are saying something worthwhile and trustworthy. It always works.

There are no special tips on how to trick people into sanity by not telling the truth. I don't think there can be such a thing at all. At least I haven't found it in dealing with my own students. Sometimes telling the truth is very painful to them, but they begin to realize it is the truth, and they appreciate it sooner or later.

It is also important to realize that you don't have to have control over others. You see, that is exactly the truth situation: you do not have all the answers; you are not assuming control over people. Instead, you are trying to tell the truth—in the beginning, in the middle, and at the end.

221

The Big No

THERE IS NO SPECIAL REALITY beyond reality. That is the Big No, as opposed to the regular no. You *cannot* destroy life. You cannot by any means, for any religious, spiritual, or metaphysical reasons, step on an ant or kill your mosquitoes—at all. That is Buddhism. That is Shambhala. You have to respect *everybody*. You cannot make a random judgment on that at all. That is the rule of the kingdom of Shambhala, and that is the Big No. You can't act on your desires alone. You have to contemplate the details of what needs to be removed and what needs to be cultivated.

222

Where Does Joy Come From?

When you are feeling ill and life is not pleasant, where does the smile come from? Where does the joy come from? It's a question of realizing that whatever your experience is, it is not necessarily all that solid. Things are not all that solid and substantial; there is an illusory quality to things. It is like driving through very thick, solid-looking fog: although it looks solid, still you know the fog is not a wall; you know you can just drive through. So you keep on driving, and at some point you get beyond the fog and you can see the road. You see that you are not devastated, at that point.

223

Working with Illness

When someone is ill, they may have a sense of anxiety, a sense of hope, or a sense of complete negativity. In relating to oneself or others in that situation, the main point is realizing that a person is not stuck with his or her sickness. If a person regards sickness as an enemy, then her body has no working basis to be well. She thinks her body is invaded by enemies, and she goes to the doctor to get rid of these foreigners occupying her castle. There is another problem—the concept of death as the archenemy, where we try to avoid death every minute, every second. When someone is ill, there has to be more emphasis on creating an atmosphere of health. Sickness is a message, and it can be cured if the right situation is created. Mind reflects body, and body is affected by the atmosphere. The idea is *recovering* rather than being *cured* of a particular disease. Basically, what we are talking about is connecting with a general sense of healthiness, or intrinsic goodness, in your state of mind. There is some sense of not giving up on life, but viewing every day as a constant journey, a constant challenge, and at the same time, a constant celebration.

224

Awakening Confidence

WARRIORSHIP refers to realizing the power, dignity, and wakefulness that are inherent in all of us as human beings. It is awakening our basic human confidence, which allows us to cheer up, develop a sense of vision, and succeed in what we are doing. Because warriorship is innate in human beings, the way to become a warrior—or the warrior's path—is to see who and what we are as human beings and cultivate that. If we look at ourselves directly, without hesitation or embarrassment, we find that we have a lot of strength and a lot of resources available constantly.

225

The Cosmic Wound

Although we may feel as though we're covered with a cast iron shield, a sore spot always exists in us, which is fantastic. That sore spot is known as embryonic compassion, potential compassion. At least we have some kind of gap, some discrepancy in our state of being, which allows basic sanity to shine through. Not only that, but there is also an inner wound, which is called *tathagatagarbha,* or buddha nature. Buddha nature is like a heart that is sliced and bruised by wisdom and compassion. When the external wound and the internal wound begin to meet and to communicate, then we begin to realize that our whole being is made out of one complete sore spot altogether. That vulnerability is compassion. We really have no way to defend ourselves anymore at all. A gigantic cosmic wound is all over the place—an inward wound and an external wound at the same time. Both are sensitive to cold air, hot air, and little disturbances of atmosphere which begin to affect us both inwardly and outwardly. It is the living flame of love, if you would like to call it that.

226

From Anger to Joy

A STUDENT ASKED ME how you can retrain anger into joy. The answer is: You just do it. There's no "how" particularly; there is no easy trick. If you go deeper into your anger, the sense of joy is there. The sense of joy is already there. If you go slightly deeper still, slightly further, you begin to realize you're taking the whole thing too seriously. The answer is just a question of basic exertion and realizing that you have to do it yourself; nobody can make you do this. There are no tricks for how to do it—except generally to build up your mindfulness and awareness, which builds up your basic healthy state of mind. That actually allows you to become a warrior, automatically.

227

Collective Problem Solving

When you work with others, it's important not to regard problems as monumental and not to feel defeated by them. You are not necessarily *the* problem-solving person, *the* troubleshooter. You don't have to take all the responsibility, thinking that you are going to solve the whole problem yourself. The solution might take a collective effort. You should take care of your part of the problem first. That way, at least one problem is solved, *your* problem. Then somebody else will take their turn, and solve their side of the problem.

It is like lifting a big table. You can't lift a big dining room table by yourself, but you need several people to carry it. It takes a collective effort. On the whole, you are not going to clean up or save the world by yourself, single-handedly. Although the *bodhisattva* vow to save all sentient beings is taken that way, nonetheless, you need *sangha,* community, along with your inspiration. You can lift one corner of the table. Then, when that part of the table has been lifted already, your friends can come along and do likewise, so that finally the table is moved out of the room. We need a sangha, a community, to solve larger problems. That seems to be the only way.

228

Meditation as a Process of Evolution

When we talk about stages on the path, in relationship to our meditation practice, we have a problem with the terminology. We tend to think of a staircase: You take the first step, and then you take the next step and the step after that. We might think meditation practice is like being in an elevator: As things become defined or clarified on the path, we go up in the elevator, and the numbers of each floor appear as we rise from one stage to the next. The problem is that meditation is not like progressing through stage after stage after stage. Rather, meditation is more like the process of growing up and aging. Although you may celebrate your birthday on a particular day, that doesn't mean that, when you blow your candle out at your party, you suddenly go from being two years old to being three. In growing up, there is a process of evolution, a process of development. That is precisely the issue as far as meditation practice is concerned. Meditation is not based on stages, but it is a process that takes place in you, in accordance with your life situation.

229

We Are Constantly Learning

When we become Buddhists, we become refugees: We take the refuge vow and commit ourselves to the Buddhist path. We make the preliminary decision to call ourselves Buddhists. After that we slowly begin to develop the confidence that we are not only working on ourselves but that we can also work with others. Then we take another vow, called the *bodhisattva* vow, to help sentient beings. As we proceed further, we are ready to take tantric transmission, or *abhisheka.* We are still making a journey. We might feel that we are going backward or forward—but that is simply the play of emotions. If we feel we are becoming infantile, we are learning; if we think we are an insignificant old man, we are still learning. A learning process takes place constantly, throughout the whole path.

230

Discontinuity

THERE'S A SENSE of impermanence that happens constantly, all the time. That's the starting point, to realize that you can't hang on to one continuous continuation, that things *do* change constantly, and that you have no permanent security. There's only one eternity, and that's the eternity of discontinuity.

231

Struggle Does Not Work

We know that our technology cannot shield us from war, crime, illness, economic insecurity, laborious work, old age, and death; nor can our ideologies shield us from doubt, uncertainty, confusion, and disorientation; nor can our therapies protect us from the dissolution of the high states of consciousness that we may temporarily achieve and the disillusionment and anguish that follow. But what else are we to do? In order to see for ourselves how this process works, we must examine our own experience. "But how are we to conduct the examination?" we might ask, "What method or tool are we to use?" The method that the Buddha discovered is meditation. He discovered that struggling to find answers did not work. It was only when there were gaps in his struggle that insights came to him. He began to realize that there was a sane, awake quality within him which manifested itself only in the absence of struggle. So the practice of meditation involves letting be.

232

Let It Be

You don't have to try to catch the universe in the same way that you would try to catch a grasshopper or a flea. You don't *have* to do something with what you have experienced, particularly. Why don't you let it be as it is? In fact, that might be necessary. If you want to use something, you have to let it be. You cannot drink all the water on earth in order to quench your thirst eternally. You might drink a glass of water, but you have to leave the rest of the water, rivers, and oceans so that if you are thirsty again, you can drink more. You have to leave some room somewhere. You don't have to gulp everything down. It's much nicer not to do that; in fact it is polite.

233

Not Too Tight, Not Too Loose

THERE IS A STORY regarding the Buddha which recounts how he once gave teaching to a famous sitar player who wanted to study meditation. The musician asked, "Should I control my mind or should I completely let go?" The Buddha answered, "Since you are a great musician, tell me how you would tune the strings of your instrument." The musician said, "I would make them not too tight and not too loose." "Likewise," said the Buddha, "in your meditation practice you should not impose anything too forcefully on your mind, nor should you let it wander." That is the teaching of letting the mind be in a very open way, of feeling the flow of energy without trying to subdue it and without letting it get out of control, of going with the energy pattern of mind. This is meditation practice.

234

The Tiger

A TIGER in its prime moves slowly but heedfully through the jungle. In this case, the tiger is not searching for prey. He is not stalking in the jungle, hoping to pounce on other animals. Rather, the image of the tiger expresses a combination of self-satisfaction and modesty. The tiger walks slowly through the jungle, with mindfulness. But because the tiger likes his body and his bounciness and sense of rhythm, he is relaxed. From the tip of his nose to the tip of his tail, there are no problems. His movements are like waves; he swims through the jungle. So his watchfulness is accompanied by relaxation and confidence. This is the analogy for the warrior's confidence.

235

Unconditional Freedom

FREEDOM—UNEXPECTED, undemanded freedom. Freedom cannot be bought or bartered for. Freedom doesn't come cheap or expensive. It just happens. It is only without any reference point that freedom can evolve. That is why it is known as freedom—because it is unconditional. So it is our duty—in fact, we might even go as far as to say it is the purpose of our life—it is our heroic duty to encourage the notion of freedom as it is, without contamination by any further pollution of this and that and that and this. No bargaining.

We have to maintain ourselves in an erect posture in order to work with freedom. The practice of meditation in the Buddhist tradition is extremely simple, extremely erect, and direct. There is a sense of pride in the fact that you are going to sit and practice meditation. When you sit and practice meditation, you don't do anything at all. You just sit and work with your breathing, your posture. You just sit and let all these thoughts come alive. You let your hidden neurosis come through. Let the discipline evolve itself.

236

One Thing at a Time

Two things cannot happen at once; it is impossible. It is easy to imagine that two things are happening at once, because our journey back and forth between the two may be very speedy. But even then we are doing only one thing at a time. The idea of mindfulness of mind is to slow down the fickleness of jumping back and forth. We have to realize that we are not extraordinary mental acrobats. We are not all that well trained. And even an extraordinarily well-trained mind could not manage that many things at once—not even two. But because things are very simple and direct, we can focus on, be aware and mindful of, one thing at a time. That one-pointedness, that bare attention, seems to be the basic point.

237

Humbleness Is the Dwelling Place

It has been said that "Humbleness is the dwelling place of the forefathers." Humbleness is the best moderator of your studentship. You might think that you are going to become the greatest yogi, or the greatest teacher, that you are going to teach and proclaim your dharma to the rest of the world. You think that, when you become the greatest yogi, you are going to fly over New York City and Chicago and compete with the airplanes. You think you will levitate and perform miracles all over the place. But those discursive thoughts don't help; humbleness is always the best and the safest. Humbleness rouses you to give birth to realization, because it allows you to hear and experience properly, without anything occupying your being. Your whole being is completely empty and waiting for the teachings to enter into you. If arrogance enters into your being, there is no room for humbleness, and the teachings have no room to enter. Moreover, when you are arrogant rather than humble, there is room for distorting the teacher or editing the teachings. It is possible to become deaf and dumb as a result of arrogance. While you carry the burden of arrogance, you will not have any form of joy. It is time to create humbleness by means of the discipline of sitting properly and thoroughly.

238

Enlightened Heart

BODHI MEANS "awakened," which is the same notion as *buddha. Bodhi* and *buddha* have the same connotation. *Chitta* means "heart." So *bodhichitta* means "awakened heart." That is what we want to plant in our mind, in our existence, altogether. Sometimes, the heart comes first: chitta comes first; and then bodhi comes later. The heart awakens, as it were. To begin with, we develop heart, heart that is not connected with egohood, personal longevity, personal entertainment, or personal egotism of any kind. We begin to develop that particular kind of heart. And that kind of heart begins to transmit the vision of heart, which is enlightened heart. So first we develop heart; then we develop what heart is all about—enlightened heart. Enlightened heart is expansive and awake. It does not demand any kind of territoriality. It does not demand that we organize or create a flock of our own egotistic companions around us; we don't have to collect tribes of followers around us. When we begin to look into those two situations—basic wakefulness and the basic lack of any need to recruit support for our own territoriality—we begin to find ourselves having a taste of enlightenment for the very first time.

239

One Version of Infinity

YOU RUN SO FAST, round and round and round, that finally the fastest way to run is to stay still. You run so fast that you begin to see your own back, and you begin to become still. At that point, the whole thing begins to become infinite. When you hold still, you supersede any kind of speed at all. You become the ultimate and utmost winner of that particular race. From that point of view, being back to square one is one version of infinity. In this case, back to square one is the infiniteness of immense immeasurable space and expansion that you experience. Therefore, it is absolutely absurd to try to search further—and the only way not to search further is to be, to stay, to stand, or sit still.

240

Conquering Cowardice

Cowardice is the seductive and distracting quality of our wandering or neurotic minds, which prevents us from resting in our natural state, the state of unwavering wakefulness that we have called the warrior's confidence. Cowardice is actually the force of evil that obstructs what we could call our basic goodness, our inherent state of confidence which is by nature devoid of cowardice and aggression, free from evil. From that point of view, the purpose of warriorship is to conquer the enemy, to subjugate the evil of our cowardly minds and uncover our basic goodness, our confidence.

241

Know Yourself

In order to understand the interpersonal situation correctly, you have to know yourself in the beginning. Once you know the style of the dynamics of your own mind, then you can begin to see how that style works in dealing with others. And, in fact, on the basis of knowing yourself, the interpersonal knowledge comes naturally. You discover that somebody has developed his or her own mind. Then you can experience how the two minds interact with each other. This leads to the discovery that there is no such thing as outside mind and inside mind at all. So "mind" is really two minds meeting together, which is the same mind in some sense.

242

We Live at the Expense of Others

We may try to be a spiritually inclined person who does not care about money. We want to be free of worldly concern. However, trying to lead life completely free from money or materialism lacks clarity and real feeling. Particularly in this highly organized society, we live at the expense of others. Whether we are in a remote place, such as the north of Scotland, or wherever we are, we still need food, and this food is produced by somebody. It is the product of someone's work. Someone has gone to a great deal of trouble to produce our food. Some people may spend their lives churning milk in order to produce butter. Some people spend their lives screwing bolts into things. Most of their lives are spent doing that. People are trained to do regular, ordinary work, and they do it.

When the time comes to retire, they feel something is missing, something has been lost. Those people suffer, but they don't dwell on suffering or pain. They have so bravely accepted their lives and ignored other aspects of life. They close one eye and just do it, just one thing. The world is made out of this, the present world anyway. Perhaps it has always been this way. This is not a question of money alone, but appreciating the practicality of life and having compassion. There is a limit to how much freedom we take.

243

Earth Is My Witness

At the dawn of his enlightenment, someone asked the Buddha, "What are your credentials? How do we know that you are enlightened?" He touched his hand to the ground. "This solid earth is my witness. This solid earth, this sane earth, is my witness." Sane and solid and definite, no imaginings, no concepts, no emotions, no frivolity, but being basically what is: this is the awakened state. And this is the example we follow in our meditation practice.

244

Sacred Action

We should regard everything that we do as very important—not a big deal, but very important. Whatever we do is sacred action. Sacred action is not necessarily something magical or god-ridden. It is the possibility that whatever we do could be *shamatha-vipashyana*-ridden, ridden with mindfulness and awareness. There is always room for precision. There are always vipashyana possibilities, possibilities of awareness, in whatever we do. Nothing is regarded as unsuitable, which is very helpful. So please pay attention to everything. When we don't let hope and fear, liking or disliking, come into the picture; when we actually taste the bread and butter in our mouth; when we don't let passion and aggression enter into it; at that point, we have the perfect opportunity for realizing awareness. Then, eating a good piece of bread with nice butter on it does not produce any karmic seeds or debts. That is how, even at this level, we can actually reduce samsaric, confused possibilities, and free ourselves from future karmic possibilities.

245

Always Now

We should not ignore the contributions of the past. The failure to appreciate the resourcefulness of human existence—which we call basic goodness—has become one of the world's biggest problems. However, we need to find the link between tradition and the present experience of life. *Nowness,* or the magic of the present moment, is what joins the wisdom of the past with the present. When you appreciate a painting, a piece of music, or a work of literature, no matter when it was created, you appreciate it *now.* You experience the same nowness in which it was created. It is always *now.*

246

Open House

THOSE WHO WANT TO PRACTICE are invited to take part in meditation, to go through the pain, go through the bliss, whatever you experience. Creating an open house situation for the practice of meditation is a gesture proclaiming that our aim and object are not related with dogma but on trying to encompass all areas of openness. That knowledge can be found throughout the teachings of Tibetan Buddhism or Buddhism in general—Sanskrit Buddhism, Pali Buddhism, or other schools of Buddhism. Since it is known that all dharmas are marked with emptiness, therefore all dharma is marked with openness, at the same time. There is tremendous room to work with chaos or confusion.

247

Dare to Let Go

In the practice of meditation, the way to be daring, the way to leap, is to disown your thoughts, to step beyond your hope and fear, the ups and downs of your thinking process. You can just be, just let yourself be, without holding on to the constant reference points that mind manufactures. You do not have to get rid of your thoughts. They are a natural process; they are fine; let them be as well. But let yourself go out with the breath, let it dissolve. See what happens. When you let yourself go in that way, you develop trust in the strength of your being and trust in your ability to open and extend yourself to others. You realize that you are rich and resourceful enough to give selflessly to others, and as well, you find that you have tremendous willingness to do so.

248

Open Your Mind

THE MORE YOU LEARN about your own mind, the more you learn about other people's minds. You begin to appreciate other worlds, other people's life situations. You are learning to extend your vision beyond what is just there in your immediate situation, on the spot, so your mind is opened that much more. And that reflects on your work with others. It makes you more skillful in deeds and also gives you more of a sense of warmth and compassion, so you become more accommodating of others.

249

The Torch of Wisdom

It is necessary to light the torch of wisdom to illuminate the thick black fog of materialism. One of the greatest teachings of Buddhism is that which transcends this and that, or the dualistic barrier. This is often described as the sword of Manjusri, the *bodhisattva* who personifies transcendental wisdom. This sword cuts the aorta of ego.

In talking about great wisdom, the most misguided remark that has been heard is that enlightenment could be manufactured by external means. That is the question: whether an experience such as transcendental knowledge can be achieved by external means or logical means or concepts—or whether it is something that we have to cultivate within ourselves. It seems that there is no other way than to work through the natural situation of daily existence. Hope, fear, pain, pleasure, misery, bliss: these dichotomies constantly go on. In order to transcend them, we have to use them as stepping-stones, without relying on heretical ideas that enlightenment could be achieved by external means. Something has to develop within ourselves.

250

The Essence of Peace

There are so many ways of interpreting and categorizing peace. We should try to look for the actual reality of peace and pass beyond the philosophical or theoretical aspects. Peace is not indulging ourselves in joy or happiness. It also isn't a state where there's no emotion, a state where there is no feeling, a state where there is no energy, either. Rather, peace is the source of everything, it is what we are, what is. One might say peace is a childlike state, the state we are born from, the primeval state, before we have been indoctrinated by anything. We might see it as some kind of ultimate mystical experience, but it is not mystical experience. Peace is that which remains both still and active and that which radiates, full of life. Because of it, people feel peaceful and open. It is a state where there is no idea of defending or trying to preserve oneself. In the Buddhist scriptures, one finds the term *tathagatagarbha,* which is buddha nature or the essence of mind. It is also described as the undisturbed color, the undisturbed texture, character, and quality of mind. One is able to bring this into consciousness through the practice of meditation. First of all, then, peace is a discovery within oneself.

251

Fearless Dharma

BUDDHA'S PROCLAMATION of emptiness is what is known as the Lion's Roar. That is the fundamental message proclaimed by the conch shell of dharma, the trumpet of dharma, the gong of dharma. With the understanding of emptiness, the light of dharma shines constantly, because there is nothing to defeat; there are no ideas to be defeated by. So the proclamation of dharma is fearless.

252

Conquering without Aggression

WHEN WE TALK about conquering the enemy, it is important to understand we are not talking about aggression. The genuine warrior does not become resentful or arrogant. Such ambition or arrogance would be simply another aspect of cowardly mind, another enemy of warriorship in itself. So it is absolutely necessary for the warrior to subjugate her own ambition to conquer at the same time that she is subjugating her other more obvious enemies. Thus the idea of warriorship altogether is that, by facing all our enemies fearlessly, with gentleness and intelligence, we can develop ourselves and thereby attain self-realization.

253

Relating to Others

We are constantly trying to work out our relation to the other. It's like your dog meeting somebody else's dog. There is a growl, a sniff, a step forward, a potential rejection, or maybe an acceptance. That kind of thing is constantly taking place. Dogs do it very generously. As far as we human beings are concerned, obviously we are more subtle, but we are less generous because we have more "me."

254

Marriage

When you get married you shouldn't expect anything at the beginning, but you should try to work together with your husband or wife. Basically speaking, marriage is a joint effort of trying to solve one another's problems, and trying to make a creative world. As long as you are not immediately looking for an ideal, happy life, you can work with marriage. On the other hand, the idea of working with problems all the time can be overwhelming. It is a question of intelligence on both sides, and at the same time, there is a need for tremendous awareness and mindfulness. Each communication that takes place between the two of you has to be sacred in some sense. You should regard your partner as a spiritual friend of some type, and try to work along with that. When there is that kind of working basis taking place, I don't see any particular obstacles.

The relationship might change anywhere: right at the beginning, or halfway through. It may not always be the same kind of relationship, because each one of you begins to grow up. So it might take a different shape; it might produce different kinds of phenomena. Nonetheless, it is workable, as long as there is a dharmic connection, a spiritual connection.

255

When You're Hassled

A STUDENT once asked me, "How is it possible to work quickly and still have any sanity about it?" When you are being hassled, you are reduced into a pinpoint, usually. You begin to become so small that you are hassled by the giant situations that begin to close in on you. You are afraid about your timetable, scheduling, and everything. Whereas if you take a greater view at that point, then you are no longer that small. You can cover a lot of areas. You can extend your tentacles greater that way, so that you have some sort of stronghold, or at least some kind of clear vision of where you're coming from. You are not just being bounced back and forth like a ping-pong ball by the mercy of the situation on your ping-pong table. When you're hassled, there's a tendency to become small. So the opposite approach, in this case, is that when you're hassled, you have to become bigger, so you can't be bounced around.

256

Sacredness versus Superstition

THERE IS A GREAT DEAL of difference between sacredness and superstition. Superstition is believing something that you've been told, such as that if somebody drops a rotten egg on your head, it is bad luck. Superstition has no foundation in basic practice. Sacredness, however, is like the experience when you look at pure gold: you get some transmission of pure goldness because gold *is* pure and good. Similarly, when you converse with a person of great wisdom, the conversation doesn't necessarily have to be profound per se—it could just be "hello" and "good-bye"—but you experience the basic nature of goodness coming out of that person. Sacredness is like putting on a fur coat in the biting cold of winter. Sacredness fulfills its purposes, and it also brings cheerfulness and goodness into our system so that we don't pollute the world. Sacredness is what allows us to say that the Shambhala principles can create an enlightened society.

257

Switching Our Allegiance

Becoming a warrior means that we can look directly at ourselves, see the nature of our cowardly mind, and step out of it. We can trade our small-minded struggle for security for a much vaster vision, one of fearlessness, openness, and genuine heroism. This doesn't happen all at once but is a gradual process. Our first inkling of that possibility comes when we begin to sense the claustrophobia and stuffiness of our self-imposed cocoon. At that point, our safe home begins to feel like a trap and we begin to sense that an alternative is possible. We begin to have tremendous longing for some kind of ventilation, and finally we actually experience a delightful breath of fresh air coming into our stale nest. At this point, we realize that it has been our choice all along to live in this restrictive, and by now somewhat revolting, mentality of defensiveness and cowardice. Simultaneously, we realize that we could just as easily switch our allegiance. We could break out of our dark, stuffy prison into the fresh air where it is possible for us to stretch our legs, to walk, run, or even dance and play. We realize that we could drop the oppressive struggle it takes to maintain our cowardice, and relax instead in the greater space of confidence.

258

Spontaneity without Qualification

WHEN YOU TAKE the *bodhisattva* vow to help others and put them before yourself, at this point, spontaneity without qualification arises in you; it is basic gentleness and basic peacefulness. You begin to realize that you can love yourself genuinely, without qualification. It is simply being there. The process of being there contains anti-ego. It contains peace, because at last you have decided to give in to something extraordinarily simple and ordinary and basic—almost at the level of naïveté.

259

The Environment around the Breath

As far as Buddha was concerned, at the point of his enlightenment, it was not the message but the implications that were more important. And as followers of Buddha, we have this approach, which is the idea of *vipashyana,* literally meaning "insight." Insight is relating not only with what you see but also with the implications of it, the totality of the space and objects around it. Breath is the object of meditation, but the environment around the breath is also part of the meditative situation.

260

Sudden Enlightenment

PEOPLE TALK about sudden enlightenment, a sudden glimpse, *satori*. So-called sudden enlightenment needs enough preparation for it to be sudden. Otherwise, it can't happen. If you have a sudden accident in your car, you have to be driving it. Otherwise, you can't have the accident. When we talk about sudden flashes, we are talking in terms of *conditional* suddenness, conditional sudden enlightenment.

Sudden enlightenment depends on the slow growth of the spiritual process, the growth of commitment, discipline, and experience. This occurs not only in the sitting practice of meditation, but also through life experiences: dealing with your wife, husband, kids, parents, job, money, sex life, emotions—everything in life. You have to learn from situations. Then, the gradual process of spiritual development is almost inevitable.

Scholastically and experientially there is no such thing as sudden enlightenment in Buddhism. It is simply the insight, or understanding, that arises from what we have already experienced. You might say, "Suddenly I saw the sunrise." But what you are seeing depends on the situation that already exists. You are just making it sound dramatic. The sun doesn't suddenly rise or set, although you may suddenly notice that it's going to happen.

261

The Snow Lion

For the Shambhala warrior, the principle of perky is symbolized by the snow lion that enjoys the freshness of the highland mountains. The warrior of perky is never caught in the trap of doubt and is always joyful and artful. The snow lion is vibrant, energetic, and also youthful. She roams the highlands where the atmosphere is clear and the air is fresh. The surroundings are wildflowers, a few trees, and occasional boulders and rocks. The atmosphere is bright and new and also has a sense of goodness and cheerfulness. Being perky does not mean that one is perked up by temporary situations, but it refers to unconditional cheerfulness, which comes from ongoing discipline. Just as the snow lion enjoys the refreshing air, the warrior of perky is constantly disciplined and continuously enjoys discipline. For her, discipline is not a demand but a pleasure.

262

Basic Goodness Can Help

You should appreciate goodness, which brings joy and a sense of celebration. Your world might be falling apart. You might have tremendous financial debts, and your husband or wife might be leaving you. You might be living in a depressed ghetto, where every night there is murder and theft, and the police sirens keep you awake. In spite of all these problems, if there is some kind of inner glow and appreciation of being as a Shambhala warrior, that ideal of warriorship will help you. Think of basic goodness, which creates upliftedness constantly. The Shambhala principles are not theory or mere concept. Sadness and joy are one in basic goodness. Don't try to push out the nightmare and don't try to bring in the blissfulness. Just rest your being in a state of basic goodness. If necessary, you could say it to yourself: "basic goodness."

263

Make the First Move

USUALLY WE ARE in a stalemate with our world: "Is he going to say he is sorry to me first, or am I going to apologize to him first?" But in becoming a *bodhisattva,* one who takes a vow to help others and put them before oneself, we break that barrier: we do not wait for the other person to make the first move. We have decided to do it ourselves. People have a lot of problems and they suffer a great deal, obviously. And we have only half a grain of sand's worth of awareness of that suffering happening in this country, let alone in the rest of the world. Millions of people in the world are suffering because of their lack of generosity, discipline, patience, exertion, meditation, and transcendental knowledge.

The point of making the first move by taking the bodhisattva vow is not to convert people to our particular view, necessarily. The idea is that we should contribute something to the world simply by our own way of relating, by our own gentleness.

264

Fathers and Mothers of Shambhala

Over the centuries, there have been many who have sought the ultimate good and have tried to share it with their fellow human beings. To realize it requires immaculate discipline and unflinching conviction. Those who have been fearless in their search and fearless in their proclamation belong to the lineage of master warriors, whatever their religion, philosophy, or creed. What distinguishes such leaders of humanity and guardians of human wisdom is their fearless expression of gentleness and genuineness—on behalf of all sentient beings. We should venerate their example and acknowledge the path that they have laid for us. They are the fathers and mothers of Shambhala, who make it possible, in the midst of this degraded age, to contemplate enlightened society.

265

A Tradition of Openness

TAKING THE *bodhisattva* vow to help others implies that instead of holding our own individual territory and defending it tooth and nail, we become open to the world that we are living in. It means we are willing to take on greater responsibility, immense responsibility. In fact, it means taking a big chance. But taking such a chance is not false heroism or personal eccentricity. It is a chance that has been taken in the past by millions of bodhisattvas, enlightened ones, and great teachers. So a tradition of responsibility and openness has been handed down from generation to generation, and now we too are participating in the sanity and dignity of this tradition.

266

The Family of Buddhas

It is not a hard-core, incorrigible world. It can be worked with within the inspiration of the *buddhadharma,* the teachings, following the example of Lord Buddha and the great *bodhisattvas.* We can join their campaign to work with sentient beings properly, fully, and thoroughly—without grasping, without confusion, and without aggression. Such a campaign is a natural development of the practice of meditation because meditation brings a growing sense of egolessness. There is a tremendous sense of celebration and joy in finally being able to join the family of buddhas. At last we have decided to claim our inheritance, which is enlightenment. From the perspective of doubt, whatever enlightened quality exists in us may seem small-scale. But from the perspective of actuality, a fully developed enlightened being exists in us already. Enlightenment is no longer a myth: it does exist. It is workable and we are associated with it thoroughly and fully. So we have no doubts as to whether we are on the path or not. It is obvious that we have made a commitment and that we are going to develop this ambitious project of becoming a buddha.

267

Fearless No

FEARLESSNESS is extending ourselves beyond a limited view. In the *Heart Sutra,* one of the Buddha's essential teachings, it talks about going beyond. Gone beyond, or *ga-te* in Sanskrit, is the basic No. In the sutra, it says there is no eye, no ear, no sound, no smell—all of those things. When you experience egolessness, the solidity of your life and your perceptions falls apart. That could be very desolate or it could be very inspiring, in terms of *shunyata,* or the Buddhist understanding of emptiness. Very simply, it is basic No. It is a real expression of fearlessness. In the Buddhist view, egolessness is preexisting, beyond our preconceptions. In the state of egolessness everything is simple and very clear. When we try to supplement the brightness of egolessness by putting a lot of other things onto it, those things obscure its brilliance, becoming blockages and veils.

268

The Garuda

Outrageousness is symbolized by the *garuda,* a legendary Tibetan bird who is traditionally referred to as the king of birds. The garuda hatches fully-grown from its egg and soars into outer space, expanding and stretching its wings, beyond any limits. Likewise, having overcome hope and fear, the warrior of outrageousness develops a sense of great freedom. So the state of mind of outrageousness is very vast. Your mind fathoms the whole of space. You go beyond any possibilities of holding back at all. You just go and go and go, completely expanding yourself. And like the garuda king, the warrior of outrageous finds nothing to obstruct his or her vast mind.

269

Not Rejecting Our World

Without this world, we cannot attain enlightenment. Without this world, there would be no journey. By rejecting the world we would be rejecting the ground and rejecting the path. All our past history and all our neuroses are related with others in some sense. All our experiences are based on others, basically. As long as we have a sense of practice, some realization that we are treading on the path, every one of those little details, which are seemingly obstacles to us, becomes an essential part of the path. Without them, we cannot attain anything at all—we have no feedback, we have nothing to work with, absolutely nothing to work with. So in a sense all the things taking place around our world, all the irritations and all the problems, are crucial.

270

Superhuman Instinct

The usual human instinct is to feed ourselves first and only make friends with others if they can feed us. This could be called "ape instinct." But in the case of the *bodhisattva* vow, when we agree to put others first, we are talking about a kind of superhuman instinct that is much deeper and more full than that. Inspired by this instinct, we are willing to feel empty and deprived and confused. But something comes out of our willingness to feel that way, which is that we can help somebody else at the same time. So there is room for our confusion and chaos and ego-centeredness: they become stepping-stones. Even the irritations that occur in the practice of the bodhisattva path become a way of confirming our commitment.

271

Miracles

Siddhi is a Sanskrit word which means "miraculous power" or "energy." It is possible to perceive the play of energy as miraculous. When we speak of miracles, it does not mean such a thing as fire turning into water or the world turning upside down. Rather, a miracle is something happening unexpectedly, some situation developing unexpectedly. There will always be a scientific explanation. A miracle need not be illogical. It could be highly logical, highly scientific. But nonetheless it takes the form of an apparent accident. For example, our connection as author and reader could be called a miracle. Why did I alone have to come from Tibet, and why did you all have to be here, reading these words? So a siddhi is a miracle in the sense of the sudden coming together of situations, assuming the guise of "accident."

272

Conquering the Hot Dog

If you are really hungry, you have a fantastic relationship with food. Let's say it's a hot dog. For many days, you want to have a hot dog. And finally, you have a hot dog. You can actually have it on your paper dish, or whatever you have. You have a fantastic relationship with the hot dog. You eat it with complete delight and complete communication. That could be said to be very aggressive. But I don't think that's true, actually, because you have open-mindedness toward that particular hot dog. You may have designed visualizations of and devotions toward your hot dog! And you have a sense of longing, and becoming completely softened. You become softened, a soft person and a reasonable person. You have a hot dog, and you can eat that hot dog very beautifully. You hold it in your hand and you feel it. You take a bite and you chew it and feel the goodness of it at the same time. It's a very real experience. That seems to be the difference between conquering and aggression.

273

Celebrate Weak Moments

MAYBE YOU ARE not doing everything wholeheartedly and properly. Maybe you cannot make it up to the prescribed level. You can't be a good meditator all the time. You can't constantly keep up your humor all the time. You have your weak moments. Your weak moments show. Of course! Why not? That's part of the celebration. Otherwise, there's nothing to celebrate. If you don't have your weak points, what's left? Just blank white, without even a dot of ink, on the sheet of your life. You can celebrate because all kinds of things are involved with your life; therefore, it is a source of celebration. There is contrast—this and that, that and this—and things can't always be sorted out properly and put into proper perspective. So let it be that way. That seems to be the source of celebration, in fact.

274

The Sensitivity of the Warrior

If the warrior does not feel alone and sad, then he or she can be corrupted very easily. In fact, such a person may not be a warrior at all. To be a good warrior, one has to feel sad and lonely, but rich and resourceful at the same time. This makes the warrior sensitive to every aspect of phenomena: to sights, smells, sounds, and feelings. In that sense, the warrior is also an artist, appreciating whatever goes on in the world. Everything is extremely vivid. The rustling of your armor or the sound of raindrops falling on your coat is very loud. The fluttering of occasional butterflies around you is almost an insult, because you are so sensitive.

275

Confusion Is Our Working Basis

A STUDENT ONCE ASKED ME, "How do you deal with confusion? How do you use it?" Well, what else do you have? The point is that we should find some working basis as soon as possible. Confusion is the first ordinary thing; it's how to begin. I think it's very important and absolutely necessary for everyone to know that we should find a stepping-stone rather than looking for an ideal situation. People may say, "When I retire from my job, I'll build my house on a beautiful coast, plant my garden, organize my house, and *then* I'm really going to sit and meditate!" That is not quite the way to go about it. We have to do something right away.

276

Somebody Became Buddha

It's very moving to know that somebody in the past became Buddha. Two thousand five hundred years ago a guy called Siddhartha became Buddha. He actually did those things and made an enormous impact and impression on people—so enormous that we still continue to follow his way and share his ideas. It's very powerful that somebody actually achieved enlightenment and went so far as to proclaim it, and to teach, and to share his life of eighty years with his students. He spoke; he taught; and he showed us how to behave, how to handle ourselves with other people. It's an extremely powerful experience. Enlightenment is no longer a myth or concept, but something that actually did take place. It did happen—I think that is the basis of our conviction.

277

Spiritual Dynamite

THERE IS SPIRITUAL ENERGY going on that is real dynamite. Can you imagine being hit by love and hate at the same time? In crazy wisdom, we are hit with compassion and wisdom at the same time, with no chance of analyzing them. There's no time to think; there's no time to work things out at all. It is *there*—but at the same time, it isn't there. And at the same time, it is a big joke.

278

Great Eastern Sun

Normally, when you see a brilliant light, that light comes from a finite source of energy. The brightness of a candle depends on how much wax surrounds it, and the thickness of the wick. The brightness of a lightbulb depends on the electric current running through it. But the Great Eastern Sun is eternally blazing; it has no need of fuel. There actually is greater luminosity that occurs without fuel, without even a pilot light. Seeing the sacred world is witnessing that greater vision, which is there all the time.

279

Questioning

BUDDHA NATURE is not regarded as a peaceful state of mind or, for that matter, as a disturbed one either. It is a state of intelligence that questions our life and the meaning of life. It is the foundation of a search. A lot of things haven't been answered in our life—and we are still searching for the questions. That questioning is buddha nature. It is a state of potential. The more dissatisfaction, the more questions, and more doubts there are, the healthier it is, for we are no longer sucked into ego-oriented situations, but we are constantly woken up.

280

A Crash Course

PARTICULARLY IN THE Western hemisphere, when you go to a new country, you take a crash course to learn how to conduct yourself. A lot of businesspeople get into a crash course to learn how to eat with chopsticks, how to move and behave, what to eat or not eat, what to say, and whether it is polite to finish the food on your plate or leave something behind. However, when you come to a spiritual master, you don't come having had a crash course on how to handle a guru. You have already had a crash course of your own, which is your own neurosis, your confusion. That's fantastic. It's a very vivid crash course, a very good one. It's honest and genuine experience. You come along as you are.

281

Art and the Wandering Mind

If subconscious gossip is going through your state of mind, if there is a sense of wildness and your mind is constantly filled with thoughts, then it is very hard to execute a work of art. So that has to be controlled and overcome. Wandering mind can be cut through, either before or during your execution of the work of art. In fact, you can use the very process of executing the work of art as a way to cut subconscious gossip, through your commitment to the medium and to the vision that exists in you and in your work.

282

Liberated from Conventionality

GIVING BIRTH to *bodhichitta* in one's heart, buddha in one's heart, brings freedom. That is the notion of freedom in Buddhism, altogether. We are talking about freedom from the constriction of our own capabilities. It is as if we were extraordinary children, possessing all sorts of genius, and we were being undermined by the society around us, which was dying to make us normal people. Whenever we would show any mark of genius, our parents would get embarrassed. They would try to put the lid on our pot, saying, "Charles, don't say those things. Just be an ordinary person." That is what actually happens to us, with or without our parents. I don't particularly want to blame our parents; we have also been doing this to ourselves. When we see something extraordinary, we are afraid to say so; we are afraid to express ourselves or to relate to such situations. So we put lids on ourselves—on our potential, our capabilities. But in Buddhism we are liberated from that kind of conventionality.

283

Making Friends with Others

EXPANDING *maitri,* or loving-kindness, to others cuts the neurosis of wishful thinking, the idea that you should be a good person only. Maitri is *intelligent* friendliness that allows acceptance of your whole being. It doesn't exclude friend or enemy, father or mother. It does not matter whether you regard your father as a friend and your mother as an enemy, your brother as a friend and your sister as an enemy, your friend as a friend, your friend as an enemy, or your enemy as a friend. The whole situation becomes extraordinarily spacious and is suddenly workable. Maybe there is hope after all. It is delightful that you could make friends with your parents and yourself, make friends with your enemies and yourself. Something is beginning to break through. Maitri is actually becoming real rather than imaginary. It is real because we don't have any hypothesis about how a good person should be or how we should improve ourselves. It is no longer hypothetical—it is real. Relationships exist; love and hate exist. Because they exist, therefore, we are able to work with them as stepping-stones. We begin to feel that we can afford to expand, that we can let go without protecting ourselves. We have developed enough maitri toward ourselves that we are no longer threatened by being open.

284

See the World as Sacred

Usually in life, when we act, when we exist, we tend to have a very wretched and small notion of what we are doing. Sometimes, we try to be good boys and girls. We struggle, taking our journey stitch by stitch. We go to sleep at night, we get up the next day, and we struggle to lead our life. The ordinary approach to that is undignified and very small, like flat Coca-Cola. Sometimes we feel better, we try to cheer up, and it feels pretty good. But then, behind that, there is the same familiar "me" haunting us all the time. We don't have to be that way, at all. We actually could see our world as a big world and see ourselves as open and vast. We can see our world as sacred. That is the key to bringing together the sun of wisdom with the moon of wakefulness.

285

Compassion with a Thousand Arms

One often finds Avalokiteshvara, the great *bodhisattva* of compassion, portrayed as having a thousand arms and a thousand eyes, and these symbolize his innumerable activities. He took a vow to save all sentient beings. As long as there are more sentient beings and as long as there is more that needs to be done, his compassion also increases. And this shows that compassion is something within us. Where there is new suffering or a new outbreak of violence, that violence contains another eye, another hand of Avalokiteshvara. The two things always go together. There is always a kind of negative, but there is always a positive which comes with it. In this particular sense, then, one should not exclude the negative and work only for the positive, but realize that the negative contains the positive within itself. Therefore the act of compassion, the act of Avalokiteshvara, is never ending.

286

The Emotional Umbilical Cord

From the moment you are born, when you first cry and breathe free from your mother's womb, you are a separate individual. Of course, there is still emotional attachment, or an emotional umbilical cord, that connects you to your parents, but as you grow older and pass from infancy into youth and maturity, as each year passes, your attachment decreases. You become an individual who can function separate from your mother and father. Individuals can develop personal discipline so that they become mature and independent and therefore experience a sense of personal freedom. But then, once that development has taken place, it is equally important to share the comradeship of human society. This is an organic expression of the greater vision of warriorship. It is based on the appreciation of a larger world.

287

Spiritual Pizza

PEOPLE HAVE DIFFERENT EXPERIENCES of reality, which cannot be jumbled together. Invaders and dictators of all kinds have tried to make others have their experience, to make a big concoction of minds controlled by one person. But that is impossible. Everyone who has tried to make that kind of spiritual pizza has failed. So you have to accept that your experience is personal. The personal experience of nowness is very much there and very obviously there. You cannot even throw it away!

288

Laziness

When people say they are bored, often they mean that they don't want to experience the sense of emptiness, which is also an expression of openness and vulnerability. So they pick up the newspaper or read anything else that's lying around the room—even reading what it says on a cereal box to keep themselves entertained. The search for entertainment to babysit your boredom soon becomes institutionalized as laziness. Such laziness actually involves a lot of exertion. You have to constantly crank things up to occupy yourself, overcoming your boredom by indulging in laziness. The remedy to that approach is renunciation. For the warrior, renunciation is giving away, or not indulging in, pleasure for entertainment's sake. We are going to kick out any preoccupations provided by the miscellaneous babysitters in the phenomenal world.

289

All-Encompassing Friendship

*M*AITRI COULD BE TRANSLATED AS "love," "kindness," or "a friendly attitude." Having a friendly attitude means that, when you make friends with someone, you accept the neurosis of that friend as well as the sanity of that friend. You accept both extremes of your friend's basic makeup as resources for friendship. If you make friends with someone because you only like certain parts of that friend, then it is not complete friendship, but partial friendship. So maitri is all-encompassing friendship, friendship which relates with the creativity as well as the destructiveness of nature.

290

A Talking Mirror

INTIMATE RELATIONSHIPS can be an important aspect of the spiritual path. At some point, your partner or mate becomes a spokesman of the universe to you, because your mate or your friend has been with you for a long time, so he or she has knowledge of you from the inside out. I think a marriage situation is extremely creative from that point of view. There is the sense of understanding that somebody is actually a talking mirror who minds your business.

291

Wisdom Cannot Be Born from Theory

WISDOM CANNOT BE BORN from theory; it must be born from your actual state of mind, which is the working basis for all spiritual practice. The wisdom of dealing with situations as they are, and that is what wisdom is, contains tremendous precision that could not come from anywhere else but the physical situations of sight, smell, feeling, touchable objects, and sounds. The earthy situation of actual things as they are is the source of wisdom. You can become completely one with smell, with sight, with sound, and your knowledge about them ceases to exist; your knowledge becomes wisdom.

292

An Open Commitment

If a person realizes that a whole chain reaction of incidents brought him into the present situation, that solves a lot of problems. It means that you have already made a commitment to whatever you are doing and the only way to behave is to go ahead, rather than hesitating constantly in order to make further choices. It is like knowing that a certain restaurant serves a particular dish that you have in mind to eat. Rather than wasting a lot of time reading the menu after you have sat down in the restaurant, go ahead and order that dish and eat it. In a sense it is a time-saving device to know that the incidents that happen in the round of life are constantly creating a particular unique situation. This is a very powerful insight which brings us a sense of freedom. It is knowing that at one and the same time you are not committed to the present situation and you are committed to it. But what we do with the present situation as it relates to the future is completely up to us. It is an open situation.

293

The Wind of Awareness

In talking about open mind, we are referring to a kind of openness that is related with letting self-existing awareness come to us. Awareness is not something that needs to be manufactured: when there is a gap, awareness enters into us. So awareness does not require a certain particular effort. Awareness is like a wind. If you open your doors and windows, it is bound to come in.

294

You Don't Own Awareness

In practicing awareness in everyday life, at a certain point the wandering mind itself, the daydreaming mind itself, turns itself into awareness and reminds you. If you are completely one with the idea of awareness as being intimate, it is a true practice. This applies as long as your relationship to the idea of awareness is a very simple one and as long as your awareness practice is connected with the sitting practice of meditation. In a proper practice of awareness, the complete proper relationship is that awareness comes toward you rather than you going toward it. In other words, if awareness is not possessed or owned, then it happens. Whereas if you try to possess and own awareness, if you relate to it as "my awareness," then it runs away from you.

295

Touch and Go

THE TECHNIQUE OF MINDFULNESS of life is based on touch-and-go. You focus your attention on the object of awareness, but then, in the same moment, you disown that awareness and go on. What is needed here is some sense of confidence—confidence that you do not have to securely own your mind, but that you can tune into its process spontaneously.

296

A Balanced State of Being

It is necessary to consider the facts and patterns of life, that is, your behavior, your approach to communication, and your way of life overall. There are certain aspects of your life that are not balanced, but those things can be developed into a balanced state of being, which is the main thing that we need to achieve. Three things make for imbalance: ignorance, hatred, and desire. Now the fact is, they are not bad. Good and bad have nothing to do with this. Rather, we are dealing only with imbalance and balance. According to some traditional Chinese Buddhist sources, monks in monasteries practiced judo, karate, and other martial arts—but not in order to challenge, kill, or destroy other people. Rather, the monks used these martial arts to learn to control their minds and to develop a balanced way of dealing with situations, without involving themselves in hatred and the panic of ego. When one practices the martial arts, one appears to be engaged in aggressive activities. Nevertheless one is not fundamentally being aggressive, from the point of view of generating or acting out of hatred. The true practice of the martial arts is a question of developing a state in which one is being fully confident, fully knowing what one is and what one is trying to do. What is necessary is to learn to understand the other side of any situation, to make friends with the opponent or the problem.

297

Mindfulness, the Essence of the Here and Now

We may undertake the practice of meditation with a sense of purity or austerity. We feel that by meditating we are doing the right thing, and we feel like good boys or girls. Not only are we doing the right thing, but we are getting away from the ugly world. We are becoming pure, renouncing the world, and becoming like the yogis of the past. We don't actually live and meditate in a cave, but we can regard the corner of the room that we have arranged for meditation as a cave. This is an attempt to isolate meditation from one's actual living situation. We build up extraneous concepts and images about it. It is satisfying to regard meditation as austere and above life.

Mindfulness of life steers us in just the opposite direction. If you are meditating in a room, you are meditating in a room. You don't regard the room as a cave. If you are breathing, you are breathing, rather than convincing yourself you are a motionless rock. Your keep your eyes open and let yourself be where you are. There are no imaginations involved with this approach. If you meditate in a rich setting, just be in the midst of it. If it is a simple setting, just be in the midst of that. You are not trying to get away from here to somewhere else. You are tuning in simply and directly to your process of life. This practice is the essence of the here and now.

298

Panoramic Awareness

LIKE A GREAT RIVER that runs down toward the ocean, the narrowness of discipline leads into the openness of panoramic awareness. Meditation is not purely sitting alone in a particular posture attending to simple processes, but it is also an openness to the environment in which these processes take place. The environment becomes a reminder to us, continually giving us messages, teachings, insights.

299

Beyond Reassurance

A STUDENT ONCE ASKED ME, "How does one get away from the need for reassurance?"

Acknowledge needing reassurance, acknowledge it as an effigy that looks in only one direction and does not look around. It is an effigy with one face, possibly only one eye. It doesn't see around, doesn't see the whole situation.

Whenever you need reassurance, that means you have a fixed idea of what ought to be. And because of that, you fix your vision on one situation, one particular thing. And those situations that are not being observed because of the point of view of needing reassurance, those things that we are not looking at, are a source of paranoia. We wish we could cover the whole ground, but since we can't do that physiologically, we have to try to stick to that one thing as much as we can. So the need for reassurance has only one eye. You need to develop more eyes, rather than just a unidirectional radar system. You don't have to fix your eye on one thing. You can have panoramic vision: vision all around at once.

300

Don't Hold On

ONCE YOU HAVE the experience of the presence of life, don't hang onto it. Just touch and go. Touch that presence of life being lived, then go. You do not have to ignore it. "Go" does not mean that we have to turn our backs on the experience and shut ourselves off from it; it means just being in it without further analysis and without further reinforcement. Holding on to life, or trying to assure oneself that it is so, has a sense of death rather than life. It is only because we have that sense of death that we want to make sure that we are alive. We would like to have an insurance policy. But if we feel that we are alive, that is good enough. We do not have to make sure that we actually do breathe, that we actually can be seen. We do not have to check to be sure we have a shadow. Just living is enough. If we don't stop to reassure ourselves, living becomes very clear-cut, very alive, and very precise.

301

Fundamentally Awake

SOMETHING EXISTS in us which is basically awake, as opposed to asleep. There is something intrinsically cheerful and fundamentally pride-worthy. It is intrinsic, which is to say: without conning ourselves into it. It is one-hundred-percent gold, beyond twenty-four karat. According to the Buddhist tradition, that is what is known as buddha nature. In Sanskrit it is often referred to as *tathagatagarbha,* which means that the essence (*garbha*) of those who have already gone beyond, the *tathagatas* or buddhas, that essence exists in us. We take that attitude: that we ourselves are fundamentally awake. We ourselves are good already. It's not just potential. It's more than potential.

302

Natural Confidence

Unconditional confidence is the pragmatic aspect of tenderness. It is the action arising from the softness. It is just like watching the sun rise. First, it is very feeble and one wonders whether it will make it. And then it shines and shines. Confidence is not arrogance or pride or anything like that. Confidence is a naturally unfolding process. It's not a question of needing confidence or not needing it. It's naturally there.

303

Letting Go

Don't confuse letting go with arrogance or indulgence. For the warrior, letting go is relaxing within the discipline you have already developed, in order to experience freedom. Letting go is not enjoying yourself at other people's expense, promoting your ego and laying trips on others. Arrogance of that kind is based on fundamental insecurity, which makes you insensitive rather than soft and gentle. The confused, or setting-sun, version of letting go is to take a drunken vacation or to be wild and sloppy and do outrageous things. For the warrior, rather than getting away from the constraints of ordinary life, letting go is going further into your life. You understand that your life, as it is, contains the means to unconditionally cheer you up.

304

Enlightenment Is Irritatingly Possible

Students might find sanity too spacious, too irritating. We would prefer a little claustrophobic insanity, snug and comforting insanity. Getting into that is like crawling back into a marsupial's pouch. That's the usual tendency, because acknowledging precision and sanity is too crispy, too cool, too cold. It's too early to wake up; we'd rather go back to bed. Going back to bed is relating to the mind's deceptions, which in fact we prefer. We like to get a little bit confused and set up our homes in that. We don't prefer sanity or enlightenment in fact. That seems to be the problem rather than that we don't have it or can't get it. If we really prefer basic sanity or enlightenment, it's irritatingly possible to get into it.

305

Beyond Facing Ourselves

ONCE WE DECIDE to look at ourselves, we may experience ourselves as wretched, in the most profoundly degrading situations, or some of us may have brilliant and good situations happening, too. Whatever arises, we look at ourselves, either based on hope or fear, whatever there may be. The important point is looking at ourselves, finding ourselves, facing ourselves, giving up our privacy and inhibition. Once we have done that, we turn to the good side of things. We begin to realize that we have something in us which is fundamentally, basically good—very good. It actually transcends the notion of good or bad. Something worthwhile, wholesome, and healthy exists in us. But don't jump the gun and try to get a hold of that first. First, let's look. If we actually face ourselves properly and fully, we will find that something else exists there, something beyond facing ourselves.

306

We Are Worthy

The starting point is acknowledging that some kind of goodness exists in us. It is necessary to take that arrogant attitude, positively speaking. There is some feeling of upliftedness. We are worthy people, and we have something going for us. We are not all that totally wretched. Of course, we do have the wretched aspect that we have to face and look at. That is absolutely necessary in order to realize the other part. But they don't actually interact as counterparts. It's simply that you go through your clouds, and then you see your sun. That is the basic approach, the basic idea we should take toward the worthiness of our existence.

307

Prajna

Prajna is a state of mind in which we have complete clarity, complete certainty. Such an experience is very rare, but at the same time very precise and penetrating. It can only occur in our state of mind for, say, once in a hundred moments. Prajna simply means "transcendental knowledge." *Pra* is "transcendent," or "supreme," *jna* means "knowledge." So prajna is the wisdom of knowing; it is to know who you are and what you are.

308

Be There

Mindfulness does not mean pushing oneself toward something or hanging on to something. It means allowing oneself to be there in the very moment of what is happening in the living process—and then letting go.

309

Catching the Wind of Knowing

THE NATURE OF *prajna,* or transcendental knowledge, starts with bewilderment. It is as if we were entering a school to study a certain discipline with great, wise, learned people. The first self-conscious awareness we would have is a sense of our own ignorance, how we feel extraordinarily stupid, clumsy, and dumb. At the same time, we begin to get wind of the knowledge; otherwise we would have no reference point to experience ourselves being dumb. Strangely enough, that is the wind of prajna, transcendental knowledge. Knowing one's own stupidity is, indeed, the first glimpse of prajna, very much so. The interesting point, however, is that we cannot consistently be stupid. Our stupidity is not all that well fortified. There are certain gaps in which we forget that we are stupid and completely bewildered. Those glimpses, those gaps where we have some room—definitely that is prajna.

310

Synchronize Mind and Body

When you are completely mindful in the present moment, mind and body are synchronized. Here, synchronizing mind and body is connected with developing fearlessness, in the sense of being accurate and direct in relating to the phenomenal world. That fearless vision reflects on you as well: it affects how you see yourself. You begin to realize that you have a perfect right to be in this universe. You have looked and you have seen, and you don't have to apologize for being born on this earth. You can uplift yourself and appreciate your existence as a human being. This discovery is the first glimpse of what is called the Great Eastern Sun, which is the sun of human dignity, the sun of human power.

311

A Common Misunderstanding

A COMMON MISUNDERSTANDING is that the meditative state of mind has to be captured and then nursed and cherished. That is definitely the wrong approach. If you try to domesticate your mind through meditation—try to possess it by holding on to the meditative state—the clear result will be regression on the path, with a loss of freshness and spontaneity. If you try to hold on without lapse all the time, then maintaining your awareness will begin to become a domestic hassle. It will become like painfully going through housework. There will be an underlying sense of resentment, and the practice of meditation will become confusing. You will begin to develop a love-hate relationship toward your practice, in which your concept of it seems good, but at the same time, the demand that rigid concept makes on you is too painful.

312

Work of Art

WHAT A WORK of art is all about is a sense of delight. Touch here, touch there, delight. It is an appreciation of things as they are and of what one is—which produces an enormous spark. Something happens—clicks—and the poet writes poems, the painter paints pictures, the musician composes music.

313

You Cannot Grow if You Cut Your Roots

Respect for tradition seems to be an important part of the learning process. We can regard tradition as the foundation and stepping-stone for learning rather than something to be rejected. You cannot grow if you cut off your roots. You will become a monster, having no relationship with your environment and no possibility of cooperation with it. Cooperation with one's background, beyond personal trips, provides richness and precision rather than pure inventiveness and the glamour of newness (or the museum mentality of dwelling in the past).

The sense of total commitment to one tradition brings about the perspective and wisdom to work with ways that have developed in other traditions. Other disciplines can then be seen as process rather than purely for their end product. Having fully incorporated into one's own life experience the knowledge and discipline learned through one tradition, you can then see the essential meaning of other traditions. When you are willing to let go and relax with experiences, not holding on to the sense of security in what you know, information becomes part of the learning process, and cooperation develops naturally.

314

Tricked into Enlightenment

When we acknowledge sanity, the basic wisdom of our state of being, then sanity comes about by itself. Acknowledging sanity can be a pretense or a discipline: you pretend to be the Buddha; you believe you *are* the Buddha. Again, we are not talking about buddha nature as an embryonic state, but of the living situation of buddhahood having already happened. We adopt such a pretense at the beginning, or maybe we should call it belief. It is a belief in the sense that our buddhahood is seemingly not real but we take it as a reality. Some element of mind's trickery is necessary. And then we find ourselves having been tricked into enlightenment.

315

Orderly Chaos

THE IDEA OF MANDALA might seem extraordinarily abstract. We need some working basis or way of identifying ourselves with the basic mandala principle. We have to see how the mandala principle is connected with a learning process or a practicing process. The word *mandala* literally means "association," or "society." The Tibetan word for mandala is *kyilkhor. Kyil* means "center," and *khor* means "fringe," "gestalt," or "area around." It is a way of looking at situations in terms of relativity: if that exists, this exists; if this exists, that exists. Things exist interdependently, and that interdependent existence of things happens in the fashion of orderly chaos.

We have all kinds of orderly chaos. We have domestic orderly chaos and we have the emotional orderly chaos of a love affair. We have spiritual orderly chaos, and even the attainment of enlightenment has an orderly chaos of its own. So mandala is a question of relating with different kinds of orderly chaos. We cannot discuss the higher mandala principle until we have some realization concerning the samsaric or confused mandala, the confused level of orderly chaos. The idea is not so much to make things harmonious and less active, but to relate with what is happening, with whatever struggles and upheavals are going on.

316

Back to Square One

Obviously, we must think first before we do. But the question is more complex: how to think, what to think, why to think, what is "to think"? No one can stop or control your thought process or your thinking. You can think anything you want. But that doesn't seem to be the point. The thinking process has to be directed into a certain approach. That does not mean that your thinking process should be in accord with certain dogma, philosophy, or concepts. Instead, one has to know the thinker itself. So we are back to square one, the thinker itself: who or what thinks and what is the thought process?

At this point the only genuine ground we have is back to square one. If you cut all kinds of roots and fascinations, all kinds of entertainment, regarding it as a very subtle form of conmanship, what do you have? You might say nothing. But it's not quite nothing—it's back to square one. The point is that your genuine existence and expressions should not be colored by any form of artificiality. However subtle, however magnificent, however beautiful or holy it may be, it still discolors your existence. So if you have a sense of ultimate cynicism, you are back to square one. If you see through any preconceptions that are laid on you, or anyone trying to influence you, if you see through how you yourself are influencing somebody else's ideas or borrowing ideas and concepts from somebody else—then you are back to square one.

317

Start with Ego

Ego is, in a sense, a false thing, but it isn't necessarily bad. You have to start with ego, and use ego, and from there it gradually wears out, like a pair of shoes. But you have to use it and wear it out thoroughly, so it is not preserved. Otherwise, if you try to push ego aside and start perfectly, you may become more and more perfect in a rather one-sided way, but the same amount of imperfection is building up on the other side, just as creating intense light creates intense darkness as well.

318

Leaving the Cocoon

When you are in your comfortable cocoon of habitual tendencies, occasionally, you shout your complaints to the outside world, such as: "Leave me alone!" "Bug off!" "I want to be who I am." Your cocoon is fabricated out of tremendous aggression, which comes from fighting against your environment, your parental upbringing, your educational upbringing, your upbringing of all kinds. You don't really have to fight with your cocoon. You can raise your head and just take a little peek out of the cocoon. Sometimes, when you first peek your head out, you find the air a bit too fresh and cold. But still, it is good. It is the best fresh air of spring or autumn or, for that matter, the best fresh air of winter or summer. So when you stick your neck out of the cocoon for the first time, you like it in spite of the discomfort of the environment. You find that it's delightful. Then, having peeked out, you become brave enough to climb out of the cocoon. You sit on your cocoon and look around at your world.

319

Panoramic Awareness in Everyday Life

In addition to the sitting form of meditation, there is the meditation practice in everyday life of panoramic awareness. This particular kind of practice is connected with identifying with the activities one is involved in. This awareness practice could apply to making artwork or doing any other activity. It requires confidence. Any kind of activity that requires discipline also requires confidence. You cannot have discipline without confidence; otherwise it becomes a sort of torturing process. If you have confidence in what you are doing, then you have real communication with the things you are using, with the material you are using. Working that way, a person is not concerned with producing masterpieces. He is just involved with the things that he is doing. Somehow the idea of a masterpiece is irrelevant.

320

The Survival Instinct

There is a level of raw anxiety about survival that manifests in us constantly, second by second, minute by minute. You breathe for survival; you lead your life for survival. The feeling is constantly present that you are trying to protect yourself from death. Instead of regarding this survival mentality as something negative, instead of relating to it as ego-clinging, here the survival struggle is regarded as a stepping-stone in the practice of meditation. Whenever you have the sense of the survival instinct functioning, that can be transmuted into a sense of being, a sense of having already survived. Mindfulness becomes a basic acknowledgment of existing. In this way, meditation becomes an actual part of life, rather than just a practice or exercise. It becomes inseparable from the instinct to live that accompanies all one's existence. That instinct to live can be seen as containing awareness, meditation, mindfulness. It constantly tunes us into what is happening. So the life force that keeps us alive and that manifests itself continually in our stream of consciousness itself becomes the practice of mindfulness.

321

Making Friends with the Real World

In the practice of meditation, having developed a sense of trust in oneself, slowly that expands its expression outward, and the world becomes a friendly world rather than a hostile world. You could say that you have changed the world: you have become the king or queen of the universe. On the other hand, you can't exactly say that, because the world has come toward you, to return your friendship. It tried all kinds of harsh ways to deal with you at the beginning, but finally the world and you begin to speak with each other, and the world becomes a real world, a completely real world, not at all an illusory world or a confused world. It is a real world. You begin to realize the reality of elements, the reality of time and space, the reality of emotions—the reality of everything.

322

The Most Enlightening Choices

RELATING WITH THE PRESENT moment is difficult and painful in many cases. Although it is straightforward, a straight road, it is quite a painful one. It is like the *bardo,* or after-death, experiences mentioned in *The Tibetan Book of the Dead.* You have a brilliant light coming at you with the image of a certain *tathagata,* or buddha, peering at you from within it. And on the side there is a less brilliant, less irritating light. The light from the side is much more beautiful because it is less glaring, only a reflection of the tathagata. So there are two choices. Should we go into the irritating one or should we just turn off on one of the sidetracks? This symbolism from *The Tibetan Book of the Dead* is very profound for our actual, everyday life situation. Perhaps the after-death experience just typifies the kind of situation in which choices are most enlightening or stimulating and most immediate. In our ordinary life situation, we have to open ourselves and investigate and then make a commitment. Without choice, there would be no leap and no moment of letting go at all. Because of choice, therefore, there is a moment of leaping and letting go happens. So it seems that it is not particularly comforting and blissful and easy. On the other hand, it could be inspiring.

323

The Joke Is on Us

IN ORDER TO BECOME a follower of the dharma, one has to become nonaggressive, to move beyond aggression. In order to do that, there has to be some kind of warmth in oneself, gentleness in oneself, which is known as *maitri,* and there has to be greater gentleness toward others, which is known as *karuna,* or compassion. When we begin to make a connection to dharma, we are willing to open our gates, to tear down our walls. Then for the first time we begin to realize that the joke has been on us all the time. Accumulating ammunition and building fence after fence was our preoccupation. It wasn't based on something actually having taken place. We have wasted so much of our energy on that. When we begin to realize the joke was on us and created by us, then we are actually following the dharma, following our minds according to the dharma.

324

Bank of Cloudy Mind

MEDITATION PROVIDES A GAP, which creates a sort of chaos in the psychological process, chaos in the mechanism of building up karmic situations. That chaos helps to see what is underneath all these thought patterns, both of the explicit and subconscious types. It begins to reveal what is underneath, which at this point is the collection of hidden suppressed thoughts. Any kind of thing that you wanted to ignore, did not want to encourage, or are ashamed about is put into this bank of confusion—the cloudy mind. The cloudy mind acts as a container for these collections of thoughts. Ashamed thoughts, irrelevant thoughts, all sorts of unwanted material have been put aside there. And meditation provides the situations which bring these thoughts up, because meditation goes right through the thought patterns and touches the ground of cloudy mind. In this way the bank is broken open, the container is broken open.

325

Square Zero

EVERYBODY HAS THEIR OWN SQUARE ONE, and they get back to it. That seems to be a universal thing. We want to be something, right? Even if we are back to square one, we are there, we are something. We don't want to be nothing, and we constantly avoid that. That is the problem. So the only alternative—not even alternative, but only choice, so to speak—is to be zero.

So square one is the basic ground from which we function, and square zero seems to be beyond even our functioning: Isness, without any definitions. It is not so much branching out, but branching in. You achieved your identity at square one, and that seems to be the problem. So ultimately one has to return to zero. Then you begin to feel that you can move around. You can do a lot of things, not be numbered. You're not subject to your own numbers, and you are not confined to a pigeonhole. So your situation could be improved if you know you have nothing but zero, which is nothing. There's no reference point anymore, just zero. Try it. It is an expression of immense generosity and immense enlightenment.

326

Meditation Is Not Separate from You

MEDITATION should not be regarded as a learning process. It should be regarded as an experiencing process. You should not try to learn from meditation but try to feel it. Meditation is an act of nonduality. The technique you are using should not be separate from you; it is you, you are the technique. Meditator and meditation are one. There is no relationship involved.

327

Don't Freeze Windhorse into Ice

YOU SHOULD APPRECIATE YOURSELF, respect yourself, and let go of doubt and embarrassment so that you can proclaim goodness and basic sanity for the benefit of others. The self-existing energy that comes from letting go is called windhorse in the Shambhala teachings. Wind is the energy of basic goodness, strong, exuberant, and brilliant. At the same time, basic goodness can be ridden, or employed in your life, which is the principle of the horse. When you contact the energy of windhorse, you can naturally let go of worrying about your own state of mind and you begin to think of others. If you are unable to let go of your selfishness, you might freeze windhorse into ice.

328

Endless Richness

If you study with a teacher who acquired his understandings by information alone, that person may tell you very wise things, beautiful things, but he won't know how to handle the gaps. He blushes or he gets embarrassed or he fidgets around between stories, between the wisdoms that he utters. But if you are dealing with somebody who is completely competent, who is actually *living* the information, the teaching has become part of her whole being, so there is no embarrassment. It goes on and on and on, like the waves of an ocean. There is endless richness. You receive a lot, but at the same time, you don't feel that she emptied out all her information to you. You feel there's much more to be said.

329

Basic Goodness Is Like a Sneeze

When we talk about basic goodness, we are not talking in terms of good and bad, but we are talking about unconditional health or unconditional goodness, without any reference point. Basic goodness is something like a sneeze. When you sneeze, there is no time to create or refer to a reference point. You just sneeze, or you just cough. Similarly, when a person has an orgasm, there's no room or time to compare that experience with anything else. That simplicity and fundamental healthiness and that capability of having your own personal experience is called basic goodness, which does not have to be compared to basic badness.

330

The Beauty of Totality

ULTIMATE GOODNESS is connected with the notion of ultimate joy without comparison to suffering. Out of that joy we begin to experience, visually, the beauty of the blue sky; the beauty of a red rose; the beauty of a white chrysanthemum; the beauty of chattering brooks; the beauty of the openness of the ocean, where sky and land meet; the beauty of sweet and sour; the beauty of music, high pitches and low; the beauty of experiencing warmth on our bodies; the beauty of cool air, which creates natural refreshment; the beauty of eating a meal when we feel hungry; the beauty of drinking water when we feel thirsty; the beauty of learning more things when we feel that we are not learned enough—when we feel that we don't know enough wisdom or vocabulary or language.

I don't want to paint a pleasure-oriented picture alone. There is also the beauty of your schoolmaster pinching you on the cheek; the beauty of being too hot on a midsummer's day; the beauty of being too cold in the middle of winter—the beauty of pain as well as the beauty of pleasure. All of those are connected with the fundamental notion of basic goodness. You might ask why we speak of beauty. The answer is that beauty here means fullness, totality—total experience. Our life is completely full even though we might be completely bored. Boredom creates aloneness and sadness, which are also beautiful. Beauty in this sense is the total experience of things as they are.

331

The Beer of Fearlessness

A WARRIOR SHOULD BE CAPABLE of artfully conducting his or her life in every action, from drinking tea to running a country. Learning how to handle fear, both how to utilize one's own fear and that of others, is what allows us to brew the beer of fearlessness. You can put all of those situations of fear and doubt into a gigantic vat and ferment them. The path of fearlessness is connected with what we do right now, today, rather than with anything theoretical or waiting for a cue from somewhere else. The basic vision of warriorship is that there is goodness in everyone. We are all good in ourselves. So we have our own warrior society within our own body. We have everything we need to make the journey already.

332

Aggression

In the state of aggression, you are constantly trying to fight with someone else. Your mind is so occupied with your opponent that you are continuously defensive, trying to defend yourself, in the fear that something will happen to you. Therefore, you are not able to see a positive alternative, one that could actually deal effectively with problems. Instead, your mind is clouded, and you do not have the clarity of mind to deal with situations. The ability to respond and act appropriately in situations has nothing to do with cranking up aggression. On the other hand, it is not particularly based on the pacifist idea of not fighting at all. We have to try to find a middle ground, where one engages the energy fully but without any aggression. The real way of the warrior is not to become aggressive and not to act against or be hostile to other people.

333

Transcendental Common Sense

IN DEALING WITH A SITUATION, the choice is there already. The way to work with that, with making that choice, is not to go according to your sense of comfort but go according to straightforwardness. If there are two choices, one is ahead of you, right in front of you, and the other choice is slightly off-center. There may be ten or twelve hundred choices, but there is one choice waiting for you on the road. The rest of them are waiting on the side, as sidetracks. It seems that the journey straight ahead is scarier, more frightening. Therefore the other choices waiting on the side become more attractive, like restaurants and drive-in movies on the side of the road. The choice has to be straightforward, based on common sense, basic sanity. Actually it is transcendental common sense.

334

Misunderstanding Awareness

Openness and awareness is a state of not manufacturing anything else; it is just being. There is a misunderstanding which regards awareness as an enormous effort—as if you were trying to become a certain unusual and special species of animal. You think now you're known as a meditator, so now you should proceed in a certain special way, and that way you will become a full-fledged meditator. That is the wrong attitude. One doesn't try to hold oneself in the state of meditation, the state of awareness. One doesn't try painfully to stick to it.

335

Distorting Dignity into Egotism

THE WESTERN TRADITION has taught us that we have a tremendous personal dignity and confidence. The distortion of this is to feel that if anything goes wrong, we can find a scapegoat somewhere outside of ourselves. We say, "This went wrong; it must be somebody's fault." When people do that consistently, then it can lead to demands for rights, riots, and all sorts of complaints, which are always based on blaming somebody else. But we never blame "me." The extreme outcome of this approach is that we feel we want to rule the world, and in doing that, we display a tremendous personal ego.

Ultimately, we could become someone like Hitler or Mussolini. These people represent the ego of an entire nation, which says, "It's not our fault. It is our nation's pride; we have our pride and glory and dignity. We are in the right." It is a gigantic ego world based on a fundamental separation from our environment. This is an extreme example, but distorting dignity into egotism can have these results.

336

The View from the Summit

The tantric journey is like walking along a winding mountain path. Dangers, obstacles, and problems occur constantly. There are wild animals, earthquakes, landslides, all kinds of things, but still we continue on our journey and we are able to go beyond the obstacles. When we finally get to the summit of the mountain, we do not celebrate our victory. Instead of planting our national flag on the summit of the mountain, we look down again and see a vast perspective of mountains, rivers, meadows, woods, jungles, and plains. Once we are on the summit of the mountain, we begin to look down, and we feel attracted toward the panoramic quality of what we see. That is *ati,* or ultimate, style. From that point of view, our achievement is not regarded as final but as a reappreciation of what we have already gone through. In fact, we would like to retake the journey we have been through.

337

Full Moon in Your Heart

The teacher, or the spiritual friend, enters your system much as medicine is injected into your veins. According to the tradition, this is known as planting the heart of enlightenment. It is transplanting the full moon into your heart. Can you imagine the full moon coming through your living room window and coming closer and suddenly entering your heart? On the one hand, unless you are terribly resentful, usually it is a tremendous relief: "Phew. The full moon has entered my heart." That's great, wonderful. On the other hand, however, when that particular full moon has entered into your heart, when it's transplanted into your heart, you might have a little panic. "Good heavens, what have I done? There's a moon in my heart. What am I going to do with it? It's too shiny!" By the way, once that moon has entered your heart, it cannot be a waning moon. It never wanes. It is always waxing.

338

Just Breathe

In the practice of meditation, simply relating with the breath is very monotonous and unadventurous—we do not discover that the third eye is opening or that chakras are unfolding. It is like a stone-carved Buddha sitting in the desert. Nothing, absolutely nothing, happens. As we realize that nothing is happening, strangely we begin to realize that something dignified is happening. There is no room for frivolity, no room for speed. We just breathe and are there. There is something very satisfying and wholesome about it. It is as though we had eaten a good meal and were satisfied with it, in contrast to eating and trying to satisfy oneself. It is a very simple-minded approach to sanity.

339

Believe in Your Basic Goodness

You don't have to feel inadequate; you just have to be. In order to do that, you need to develop an attitude of believing in your basic goodness and you need to practice meditation. When you sit like the Buddha, you begin to realize something called enlightenment. That is just realizing that there is something very straightforward and very sparkling in you. It is not necessarily feeling good. It is much better than feeling good; you have a sense of tremendous buoyancy, upliftedness. You feel healthy and simple and strong.

340

The Wisdom of Shambhala

THE BEST DOCTOR of all the doctors, the best medicine of medicines, and the best technology of technologies cannot save you from your life. The best consultants, the best bank loans, and the best insurance policies cannot save you. Technology, financial help, your smartness or good thinking of any kind—none will save you. That may seem like the dark truth, but it is the real truth. In the Buddhist tradition, this is called the *vajra* truth, the diamond truth, the truth you cannot avoid or destroy.

We cannot avoid our lives at all—young or old, rich or poor. Whatever happens, we cannot save ourselves from our lives at all. We have to face the truth—not even the eventual truth but the real truth of our lives. We are here; therefore, we have to learn how to go forward with our lives. This truth is what we call the wisdom of Shambhala.

341

The Birth of Karma

In the process of giving birth to a child, each push becomes a heroic effort. You actually have to give birth to your child, whom you want very much to get out of your body. Pushing to give birth is making a definite statement: "I am going to have this child. And I'm going to make him or her come out of my body." The push that mothers experience in labor is like the birth of karma. The birth of karma is a push to give birth to the world of passion, aggression, and ignorance. Birth is accompanied by a sense of continuity between mother and child, creator and creation. When a mother pushes and gives birth, the child that you give birth to is an extension or a continuity of you. You don't push so much because you want to get rid of this child altogether. Rather, you think, "I am going to create this new life out of my body. This particular child is going to be *my* child; I'm going to be its mother." There is a sense of ownership, a sense of continuity. In terms of karma, you feel that you are giving birth to *your* world: "This is my world; I'm going to get into this, my world."

342

True Patience

PATIENCE, *kshanti* in Sanskrit, is usually taken to mean forbearance and the calm endurance of pain and hardship. But in fact, it means rather more than that. It is forbearing in the sense of seeing the situation and seeing that it is right to forbear and to develop patience. *Kshanti* has an aspect of intelligence, in contrast, one might say, to an animal loaded with baggage who must go on and on walking along the track until it just drops dead.

That kind of patience is patience without wisdom, without clarity. In meditation, we develop patience with clarity, and energy with the eye of understanding.

343

Solidifying the Present

We have developed too much reference to time as a record of successive processes, achievements, and accomplishments that we have managed to collect. We have made something like a file out of it, a case history out of it. So our achievements have been recorded and recorded and recorded—constantly. In other words, the corpse of the present is being preserved as a record. And as we go along, we go on preserving our achievements, so that the whole process becomes more past-oriented. We have recourse to our records as a way of proving ourselves and also as a way of digging up new information. If emergency situations come up, we could reuse our old records; we could repeat them. That recording situation goes on all the time. It is solidifying the present aspect of the past.

344

Every Beat of Your Heart

You are here; you are living; let it be that way—that is mindfulness. Your heart pulsates and you breathe. All kinds of things are happening in you at once. Let mindfulness work with that, let that be mindfulness. Let every beat of your heart, every breath, be mindfulness itself. You do not have to breathe in a special way; your breath *is* an expression of mindfulness. If you approach mindfulness in this way, it becomes very personal and very direct.

345

Intrinsic Joy

A LOT OF US FEEL ATTACKED by our own aggression and by our own misery and pain. But none of that particularly presents an obstacle to creating enlightened society. What we need, to begin with, is to develop kindness toward ourselves and then to develop kindness toward others. It sounds very simple-minded, which it is. At the same time, it is *very* difficult to practice.

Pain causes a lot of chaos and resentment, and we have to overcome that. It is an extremely simple logic. Once we can overcome pain, we discover intrinsic joy, and we have less resentment toward the world and ourselves. By being here, naturally being here, we have less resentment. Resentment is not being here. We are somewhere else, because we are preoccupied with something else. When we are here, we are simply here—without resentment and without preoccupation. And by being here, we become cheerful.

346

Belief Comes from Perception

I DO NOT BELIEVE in the mystical world, the ethereal world, the world of the unseen, unknown, or whatever. There is no reason to believe in it, because we don't perceive it. Belief comes from perception. If there's no perception of something, we don't believe it. Belief does not come from manufacturing ideas. There may be millions of arguments and logics set forth, saying that there is an unseen world that operates on higher levels of consciousness, a world that fulfills human concerns, punishes those who don't believe, and so forth. But from the point of view of physics, that is unreal. I'm not going to say that there is another world. The world that we live in is the only world.

347

Give Your Goodness to Others

GIVE YOUR GOODNESS BACK to others. Let them glow. You have that much power. You can do it. You don't need to rely on anybody else's goodness. You have a resource already, which is your own goodness. You are already good, and you can actually transmit that goodness to others. In Buddhism, we call it *tathagatagarbha,* or buddha nature.

348

Free from the Hunger Inside

THERE IS A STORY from the time of Buddha of a woman who was one of the poorest beggars in India. She was poor in kind and poor in mind. She wanted so much, and this made her feel even poorer. One day she heard that Buddha was invited to Anathapindika's place in the Jeta Grove. Anathapindika was a wealthy householder and a great donor. She decided to follow the Buddha there because she knew that he would give her food, whatever was left over. She attended the ceremony of offering food to the *sangha* and to Buddha, and then she sat there waiting until Buddha saw her.

When he saw her he asked, "What do you want?" Of course, he knew, but she actually had to admit and say it. She said, "I want food. I want you to give me what is left over." Buddha replied, "In that case, you must first say no. You have to refuse when I offer it to you." He held out the food, but she found it very difficult to say no. She realized that in all her life she had never said no. Whenever anyone had anything or offered her anything, she had always said, "Yes, I want it."

After great difficulty, she finally did say no, and then Buddha gave her the food. Through this, she realized that the real hunger was her desire to own, grasp, possess, and want. This is an example of how one can practice generosity toward oneself. The point here is to free oneself from this possessiveness, this continual wanting.

349

Undoing Habitual Patterns

In order to overcome ego, we have to undo our habitual patterns, which we have been developing for thousands of years, thousands of eons, up to this point. Such habitual patterns may not have any realistic ground, but nonetheless, we have been accustomed to doing their dirty work, so to speak. We are used to our habitual patterns and neuroses at this point. We have been used to them for such a long time that we end up believing they are the real thing. In order to overcome that, to begin with, we have to see our egolessness: seeing the egolessness of oneself and the egolessness of other, and how we can actually overcome our anxiety and pain, which in Buddhist terms is known as freedom, liberation, freedom from anxiety. That is precisely what nirvana means—relief.

350

Absentminded Awareness

If we take the term in a positive and creative sense, we could say that awareness is a state of absentmindedness. The point here is that, when there is no mind to be absent, energy comes in, and so you are accurate, you are precise, you are mindful—but absentminded at the same time. So maybe we can use the term *absentminded* in this more positive sense, rather than in the conventional sense of being forgetful or constantly spaced out, so to speak. So whenever there is a message of awareness, then you are in it, you are aware already. There is the state of absentmindedness and mindfulness at the same time. Approached in this way, mindfulness is no longer a problem, a hassle, or a big deal.

351

The World Is Going to Wake Us Up

THIS WORLD NEEDS tremendous help. Everybody's in trouble. Sometimes they pretend not to be, but still, there's a lot of pain and hardship. Everybody, every minute, is tortured, suffering a lot. We shouldn't just ignore them and save ourselves alone. That would be a tremendous crime. In fact, we can't just save ourselves, because our neighbors are moaning and groaning all over the place. So even if we could just save ourselves, we wouldn't have a peaceful sleep. The rest of the world is going to wake us up with their pain.

352

Smile at Fear

When you are frightened by something, you have to relate with fear, explore why you are frightened, and develop some sense of conviction. You can actually look at fear. Then fear ceases to be the dominant situation that is going to defeat you. Fear can be conquered. You can be free from fear if you realize that fear is not the ogre. You can step on fear, and therefore you can attain what is known as fearlessness. But that requires that, when you see fear, you smile.

353

Teaching Is Learning

Teachers must be prepared to learn from pupils. That is very, very important. Otherwise there is really no progress on the part of the students, because in a sense one would be too keen and interested in the process of making the pupils receive the expansion of one's own ego and wanting to produce another you, rather than helping them to develop ability of their own. So teachers must be prepared to learn from their pupils; then there is a continual rapport. Exchanging takes place all the time; then as you teach, the pupils don't get bored with you, because you develop as well. There is always something different, something new each moment, so the material never runs out. One could apply this even to technical studies and the way of teaching things. It could be mathematics or science or anything at all. If the teacher is prepared to learn from the pupil, then the pupil also becomes eager to give, so there is real love, and real communication takes place. That is the greatest generosity.

354

Have Confidence in Awareness and Relax

THE WARRIOR'S ACCOMPLISHMENT of outrageousness is like a good, self-existing sword—desire to sharpen it will make it dull. When, out of hope and fear, you apply a competitive or comparative logic to your experience, trying to measure how much you have fathomed, how much is left to fathom, or how much someone else has fathomed, you are just dulling your sword, the sharpness of your mind. Instead, have confidence in your awareness and relax in your ability to connect with a larger vision, the experience of vast mind.

355

Work with the Present Situation

THE BUDDHIST TRADITION teaches the truth of impermanence, or the transitory nature of things. The past is gone and the future has not yet happened, so we work with what is here—the present situation. This actually helps us not to categorize or theorize. A fresh, living situation is taking place all the time, on the spot. This noncategorical approach comes from being fully here, rather than trying to reconnect with past events. We don't have to look back to the past in order to see what people are made out of. Human beings speak for themselves, on the spot.

356

Health Comes First; Sickness Is Secondary

ACCORDING to the Buddhist tradition, people inherently possess buddha nature; that is, they are basically and intrinsically good. From this point of view, health is intrinsic. That is, health comes first; sickness is secondary. Health *is.* So being healthy is being fundamentally wholesome, with body and mind synchronized in a state of being which is indestructible and good. This intrinsic, basic goodness is always present in any interaction of one human being with another.

357

Giving a Part of Oneself

You have to be fully involved; you have to become one with what you are doing. So it is with giving things away. No matter how small the thing is in terms of value, one must be fully involved in the giving, so that a part of one's ego is also given away. Through that one reaches the *paramita,* the transcendental act, of generosity, which is something beyond the ordinary. If one is able to give of one's self, ego, a part of that possessiveness and passion, then one is really practicing the dharma, the teaching of the Buddha, which is passionlessness.

358

Not Entrapped in Karma

If you are captivated by the past, then you can't make a move. But if you have the faintest, slightest doubt about your existence, the faintest suspicion that it could be changed—any progressive mentality, rebellious approach, revolutionary approach, whatever—that breeds further freedom. In other words, the potential of the embryonic enlightened mind in us can't be undermined by the heavy karma of the past all the time. Sooner or later it's going to break through. So we are not entrapped in karma, particularly. There is free choice from that point of view.

359

Buddha Wasn't a Buddhist

Helping others is a question of being genuine and projecting that genuineness to others. This way of being doesn't have to have a title or a name particularly. It is just being ultimately decent. Take the example of the Buddha himself—he wasn't a Buddhist!

360

Managing Our Life Properly

A STORY IS TOLD about Ananda, the Buddha's personal attendant, who had the desire to engage in a long period of fasting. He began to grow feeble and weak; he couldn't sit and meditate, so finally the Buddha told him, "Ananda, if there is no food, there is no body. If there is no body, there is no dharma. If there is no dharma, there is no enlightenment. Therefore go back and eat." That is the basic logic of the Buddhist teachings and of Buddhist psychology. We can actually be decent and sane on the spot, not through extreme measures but by managing our life properly, and thereby cultivating *maitri*, gentleness and friendliness to yourself.

361

Willing to Be a Fool

THERE IS LOTS OF ROOM to make mistakes. But such room for mistakes cannot be created unless there is surrendering, giving, some kind of opening. It cannot take place if there's no basis for it. However, if there is some basis—if we can give away our aggression or attempt to give it away, if we attempt to open up and strip away our territoriality and possessiveness—then there is lots of room for making mistakes. That doesn't necessarily mean there is room for dramatic mistakes, but lots of little dribbles of mistakes can take place, which usually occur in any case—we can't avoid it. We have to allow ourselves to realize that we are complete fools; otherwise, we have nowhere to begin. We have to be willing to be a fool and not always try to be a wise guy. We could almost say that being willing to be a fool is one of the first wisdoms.

362

Cosmic Pancake

OUR ORDINARY APPROACH to reality and truth is so poverty-stricken that we don't realize that the truth is not one truth, but all truth. It could be everywhere, like raindrops, as opposed to water coming out of a faucet that only one person can drink from at a time. Our limited approach is a problem. It may be our cultural training to believe that only one person can get the truth: "You can receive this, but nobody else can." There are all sorts of philosophical, psychological, religious, and emotional tactics that we use to motivate ourselves, which say that we can do something but nobody else can. Since we think we are the only one that can do something, we crank up our machine and we do it. And if it turns out that somebody else has done it already, we begin to feel jealous and resentful. In fact, the dharma has been marketed or auctioned in that way. But from the point of view of *ati,* the ultimate view, there is "all" dharma rather than "the" dharma. The notion of "one and only" does not apply anymore. If a gigantic pancake falls on our head, it falls on everybody's head. In some sense it is both a big joke and a big message. You cannot even run to your next-door neighbor saying, "I had a little pancake fall on my head. What can I do? I want to wash my hair." You have nowhere to go. It is a cosmic pancake that falls everywhere on the face of the earth. You cannot escape—that is the basic point. From that point of view, both the problem and the promise are cosmic.

363

Be There All Along

Sometimes people find that being tender and raw is threatening and seemingly exhausting. Openness seems demanding and energy consuming, so they prefer to cover up their tender heart. Vulnerability can sometimes make you nervous. It is uncomfortable to feel so real, so you want to numb yourself. You look for some kind of anesthetic, anything that will provide you with entertainment. Then you can forget the discomfort of reality. People don't want to live with their basic rawness for even fifteen minutes. For the warrior, fearlessness is the opposite of that approach. Fearlessness is a question of learning how to be. Be there all along: that is the message. That is quite challenging in what we call the setting-sun world, the world of neurotic comfort where we use everything to fill up the space.

364

Embryonic Sadness

When you are trying to help others, you begin to feel that the world is so disordered. I personally feel sadness, always. You feel sad, but you don't really want to burst into tears. You feel embryonic sadness. That sadness is a key point. In the back of your head, you hear a beautiful flute playing, because you are so sad. At the same time, the melody cheers you up. You are not on the bottom of the barrel of the world or in the Black Hole of Calcutta. In spite of being sad and devastated, there is something lovely taking place. There is some smile, some beauty. In the Shambhala world, we call that daringness. In the Buddhist language, we call it compassion. Daringness is sympathetic to oneself. There is no suicidal sadness involved at all. Rather, there is a sense of big, open mind in dealing with others, which is beautiful, wonderful.

365

Sit and Do Nothing

THE WORLD CAN BE EXPLORED; it is workable, wherever you go, whatever you do. But I would like to plant one basic seed in your mind: I feel that it is absolutely important to make the practice of meditation your source of strength, your source of basic intelligence. Please think about that. You could just sit down and do nothing. Stop acting, stop speeding. Sit and do nothing. You should take pride in the fact that you have learned a very valuable message: You actually can survive beautifully by doing nothing.

THE PRACTICE OF MEDITATION

THE PRACTICE OF MEDITATION was taught by the Lord Buddha over 2,500 years ago, and it has been part of the Buddhist and Shambhala traditions since that time. It is based on an oral tradition: from the time of the Buddha, this practice has been transmitted from one human being to another. In this way, it has remained a living tradition, so that, although it is an ancient practice, it is still up-to-date. I am going to discuss the technique of meditation in some detail here, but it is important to remember that, if you want to fully understand this practice, you need direct, personal instruction.

By meditation here we mean something very basic and simple that is not tied to any one culture. We are talking about a very basic act: sitting on the ground, assuming a good posture, and developing a sense of our spot, our place on this earth. This is the means of rediscovering ourselves and our basic goodness, the means to tune ourselves into genuine reality, without any expectations or preconceptions.

The word meditation is sometimes used to mean contemplating a particular theme or object: meditating *on* such and such a thing. By meditating on a question or problem, we can find the solution to it. Sometimes meditation also is connected with achieving a higher state of mind by entering into a trance or absorption state of some kind. But here we are talking about a completely different concept of meditation, unconditional meditation, without any object or idea in mind. Meditation is simply training our state of being so that our mind and body can be synchronized. Through the practice of meditation, we can learn to be without deception, to be fully genuine and alive.

Meditation practice begins by sitting down and assuming your seat cross-legged on the ground. You begin to feel that by simply being on the spot, your life can become workable and even wonderful. You realize that you are capable of sitting like a king or queen on a throne. The regalness of that situation shows you the dignity that comes from being still and simple.

In the practice of meditation, an upright posture is extremely important. Having an upright back is not an artificial posture. It is natural to the human body. When you slouch, that is unusual. You can't breathe properly when you slouch, and slouching also is a sign of giving in to neurosis. So when you sit erect, you are proclaiming to yourself and to the rest of the world that you are going to be a warrior, a fully human being.

To have a straight back you do not have to strain yourself by pulling up your shoulders; the uprightness comes naturally from sitting simply but proudly on the ground or on your meditation cushion. Then, because your back is upright, you feel no trace of shyness or embarrassment, so you do not hold your head down. You are not bending to anything. Because of that, your shoulders become straight automatically, so you develop a good sense of head and shoulders. Then you can allow your legs to rest naturally in a cross-legged position; your knees do not have to touch the ground. You complete your posture by placing your hands lightly, palms down, on your thighs. This provides a further sense of assuming your spot properly.

In that posture, you don't just gaze randomly around. You have a sense that you are *there* properly; therefore your eyes are open, but your gaze is directed slightly downward, maybe six feet in front of you. In that way, your vision does not wander here and there, but you have a further sense of deliberateness and definiteness.

In you daily life, you should also be aware of your posture, your head and shoulders, how you walk, and how you look at people. Even when you are not meditating, you can maintain a dignified state of existence. You can transcend your embarrassment and take pride in being a human being. Such pride is acceptable and good.

Then, in meditation practice, as you sit with a good posture, you pay attention to your breath. When you breathe, you are utterly there, properly there. You go out with the outbreath, your breath dissolves, and then the inbreath happens naturally. Then you go out again. So there is a constant going out with the outbreath. As you breathe out, you dissolve, you diffuse. Then your inbreath occurs naturally; you don't have to follow it in. You simply come back to your posture, and you are ready for another outbreath. Go out and dissolve: *tshoo;* then come back to your posture; then *tshoo* and come back to your posture.

Then there will be an inevitable *bing!*—thought. At that point, you say, "thinking." You don't say it out loud; you say it mentally: "thinking." Labeling your thoughts gives you tremendous leverage to come back to your breath. When one thought takes you away completely from what you are actually doing—when you do not even realize that you are on the cushion, but in your mind you are in San Francisco or

New York City—you say "thinking," and you bring yourself back to the breath.

It doesn't really matter what thoughts you have. In the sitting practice of meditation, whether you have monstrous thoughts or benevolent thoughts, all of them are regarded purely as thinking. They are neither virtuous nor sinful. You might have a thought of assassinating your father or you might want to make lemonade and eat cookies. Please don't be shocked by your thoughts: any thought is just thinking. No thought deserves a gold medal or a reprimand. Just label your thoughts "thinking," then go back to your breath. "Thinking," back to the breath; "thinking," back to the breath.

The practice of meditation is very precise. It has to be on the dot, right on the dot. It is quite hard work, but if you remember the importance of your posture, that will allow you to synchronize your mind and body. If you don't have good posture, your practice will be like a lame horse trying to pull a cart. It will never work. So first you sit down and assume your posture, then you work with your breath; *tshoo,* go out, come back to your posture; *tshoo.* When thoughts arise, you label them "thinking" and come back to your posture, back to your breath. You have mind working with breath, but you always maintain body as a reference point. You are not working with your mind alone. You are working with your mind and your body, and when the two work together, you never leave reality.

Condensed from "Discovering Basic Goodness," in *Shambhala: The Sacred Path of the Warrior.*

SOURCES

1. From "Sacred World," in *Shambhala: The Sacred Path of the Warrior,* Shambhala Library ed., 141. 2. From "Discovering Basic Goodness," in *Shambhala: The Sacred Path of the Warrior,* Shambhala Library ed., 21. 3. From "The Tibetan Buddhist Teachings and Their Application," in *The Collected Works of Chögyam Trungpa,* 3:521–22. 4. From Talk One of *Warriorship in the Three Yanas.* 5. From Talk One of *Warriorship in the Three Yanas.* 6. From "The Cosmic Sneeze," in *Great Eastern Sun: The Wisdom of Shambhala,* 54. 7. From "The Life and Example of Buddha," in *Meditation in Action,* 1970 ed., 12–13. 8. From "The Life and Example of Buddha," in *Meditation in Action,* 1970 ed., 13. 9. From "The Development of Ego," in *Cutting Through Spiritual Materialism,* 121–22. 10. From Talk Five of *Warriorship in the Three Yanas.*

11. From "Buddha Is Everywhere," in *Glimpses of Realization: The Three Bodies of Enlightenment,* 72–73. 12. From "The Ultimate Truth Is Fearless." 13. From "Fear and Fearlessness," in *Shambhala: The Sacred Path of the Warrior,* Shambhala Library ed., 34–35. 14. From "A Dot in the Open Sky," in *Great Eastern Sun: The Wisdom of Shambhala,* 23. 15. From "Practice and Basic Goodness: A Talk to Children," in *The Heart of the Buddha,* 193–94. 16. From "Introduction," in *Cutting Through Spiritual Materialism,* Shambhala Dragon ed., 9. 17. From "A Dot in the Open Sky," in *Great Eastern Sun: The Wisdom of Shambhala,* 23. 18. From "The Meeting of Buddhist and Western Psychology," in *The Sanity We Are Born With: A Buddhist Approach to Psychology,* 3. 19. From "Trapping the Monkey," in *The Teacup and the Skullcup: Chögyam*

Trungpa on Zen and Tantra, 72. 20. From "The True Spiritual Path," in *The Essential Chögyam Trungpa,* 46.

21. From "What Is the Heart of the Buddha?" in *The Heart of the Buddha,* 6. 22. From "Fear and Fearlessness," in *Shambhala: The Sacred Path of the Warrior,* Shambhala Library ed., 36–37. 23. From Talk One of *Meditation: The Way of the Buddha.* 24. From "The Bodhisattva Vow" in *The Heart of the Buddha,* 110–11. 25. From "The Dualistic Barrier," in *The Myth of Freedom and the Way of Meditation,* 68. 26. From "The Fourth Moment," in *Shambhala Sun* 14, no. 4 (March 2006): 43. 27. From "Lion's Roar," in *The Myth of Freedom and the Way of Meditation,* Shambhala Dragon ed., 69. 28. From "Taming the Horse, Riding the Mind," in *The Sanity We Are Born With: A Buddhist Approach to Meditation,* 16. 29. From "Boredom" in *The Myth of Freedom and the Way of Meditation,* Shambhala Library ed., 70–71. 30. From "The Star of Bethlehem" in *The Path Is the Goal: A Basic Handbook of Buddhist Meditation,* 46.

31. From "Fantasy and Reality," in *The Myth of Freedom and the Way of Meditation,* Shambhala Library ed., 3–4. 32. From "Transformation of Bad Circumstances," in *Training the Mind and Cultivating Loving-Kindness,* Shambhala Library ed., 69, 71, 72. 33. From "Natural Hierarchy," in *The Collected Works of Chögyam Trungpa,* 8:435. 34. From "Maitri Space Awareness in a Buddhist Therapeutic Community," in *The Sanity We Are Born With: A Buddhist Approach to Psychology,* 166. 35. From "The Positive Aspect of Suffering." 36. From "Green Energy," in *The Heart of the Buddha,* 208–9. 37. From "The Martial Arts and the Art of War," in *The Collected Works of Chögyam Trungpa,* 8:416–17. 38. From "Explanation of the Vajra Guru Mantra," in *The Collected Works of Chögyam Trungpa,* 5:322. 39. From "The Bardo of Dreams," in *Transcending Madness: The Experience of the Six Bardos,* 120–21. 40. From

"Anuttara Yoga," in *Journey without Goal: The Tantric Wisdom of the Buddha,* 125.

41. From "The Basic Body," in *The Lion's Roar: An Introduction to Tantra,* 48. 42. From "The Star of Bethlehem," in *The Path Is the Goal: A Basic Handbook of Buddhist Meditation,* 39. 43. From "A Golden Buddha," in *Glimpses of Mahayana* 12–13. 44. From "Work," in *Selected Community Talks,* 4. 45. From "Cool Boredom," in *Selected Community Talks,* 55. 46. From "Conquering Fear," in *The Collected Works of Chögyam Trungpa,* 8:396. 47. From "The Tibetan Buddhist Teachings and Their Application," in *The Collected Works of Chögyam Trungpa,* 3:518. 48. From "Past, Present, and Future," in *Karma,* 14. 49. From "The Tibetan Buddhist Teachings and Their Application," in *The Collected Works of Chögyam Trungpa,* 3:519. 50. From "The Positive Aspect of Suffering."

51. From "Working with Early Morning Depression," in *Great Eastern Sun: The Wisdom of Shambhala,* 27. 52. From "Heaven, Earth and Man," in *The Collected Works of Chögyam Trungpa,* 7:669. 53. From "Disappointment," in *The Myth of Freedom and the Way of Meditation,* 5. 54. From "Creating an Enlightened Society," in *Shambhala: The Sacred Path of the Warrior,* 25–27. 55. From "Conquering Fear," in *The Collected Works of Chögyam Trungpa,* 8:404. 56. From *The Warrior's Way,* 8. 57. From "Becoming a Full Human Being," in *The Sanity We Are Born With: A Buddhist Approach to Psychology,* 138–39. 58. From "Spiritual Materialism," in *Cutting Through Spiritual Materialism,* Shambhala Classic ed., 17–18. 59. From "Patience," in *Meditation in Action,* 1970 ed., 48–49. 60. From "Blamelessness: How to Love Yourself," in *Great Eastern Sun: The Wisdom of Shambhala,* 121–22.

61. From "Theism and Non-theism," in *Speaking of Silence: Christians and Buddhists in Dialogue,* 154. 62. From "The Basic Gasp of

Goodness," in *Great Eastern Sun: The Wisdom of Shambhala,* 172. 63. From "Renunciation and Daring," in *Shambhala: The Sacred Path of the Warrior,* Shambhala Library ed., 63. 64. From "Patience," in *Meditation in Action,* 1970 ed., 48. 65. From "The Martial Arts and the Art of War," in *The Collected Works of Chögyam Trungpa,* 8:417. 66. From "A New Year's Message." 67. From Talk One in *Work, Sex, and Money.* 68. From Talk One of *Work, Sex, and Money.* 69. From "Dathun Letter." 70. From "Conquering Fear," in *The Collected Works of Chögyam Trungpa,* 8:396.

71. From "Remarks at the Opening Ceremony of Samye Ling Meditation Centre in Scotland." 72. From "Mandala," in *Journey without Goal: The Tantric Wisdom of the Buddha,* 36. 73. From "Conquering Fear," in *The Collected Works of Chögyam Trungpa,* 8:399–400. 74. From "The Journey," in *The Lion's Roar: An Introduction to Tantra,* 3. 75. From "The Fool," in *The Myth of Freedom and the Way of Meditation,* 44. 76. From Chögyam Trungpa and Rigdzin Shikpo, "The Way of Maha Ati," in *The Collected Works of Chögyam Trungpa,* 1:463. 77. From "Working with Early Morning Depression," in *Great Eastern Sun: The Wisdom of Shambhala,* 30–35. 78. From "Patience," in *Meditation in Action,* Shambhala Library ed., 67. 79. From "Wash Your Dishes and Take off Your Roof," in *Glimpses of Space: The Feminine Principle and Evam,* 79–80. 80. From "How to Rule," in *Shambhala: The Sacred Path of the Warrior,* 119–20.

81. From "Challenge from a Wise Demoness," in *Songs of Milarepa.* 82. From "Dathun Letter." 83. From "Aloneness and the Virtues of the Higher Realms," in *Great Eastern Sun: The Wisdom of Shambhala,* 153. 84. From "The Four Foundations of Mindfulness," in *The Heart of the Buddha,* 43. 85. From "An Approach to Meditation: A Talk to Psychologists," in *The Sanity We Are Born With: A Bud-*

dhist Approach to Psychology, 55. 86. From "From a Workshop on Psychotherapy," in *The Sanity We Are Born With: A Buddhist Approach to Psychology,* 179. 87. From "What is the Heart of the Buddha?" in *The Heart of the Buddha,* 6–7. 88. From "The Tibetan Buddhist Teachings and Their Application," in *The Collected Works of Chögyam Trungpa,* 3:523. 89. From "The Birth of Ego," in *The Sanity We Are Born With: A Buddhist Approach to Psychology,* 78. 90. From "Dathun Letter."

91. From "Theism and Non-theism," in *Speaking of Silence: Christians and Buddhists in Dialogue,* 154. 92. From Talk One of *Work, Sex, and Money.* 93. From "One Stroke," in *Dharma Art,* 100. 94. From "Disappointment," in *Tibet Journal* 2, no. 4 (Winter 1977), 38. 95. From "Disappointment," in *Tibet Journal* 2, no. 4 (Winter 1977), 39. 96. From "Meditation," in *Dharma Art,* 21. 97. From Talk One of *Work, Sex, and Money.* 98. From Talk Five of *Warriorship in the Three Yanas.* 99. From "Disappointment," in *Tibet Journal* 2, no. 4 (Winter 1977), 40. 100. From "Vajra Nature," in *Journey without Goal: The Tantric Wisdom of the Buddha,* 26.

101. From "Vajra Nature," in *Journey without Goal: The Tantric Wisdom of the Buddha,* 26–27. 102. From "Recollecting the Present," in *The Path Is the Goal: A Basic Handbook of Buddhist Meditation,* 81–82. 103. From "Dathun Letter." 104. From "Recollecting the Present," in *The Path Is the Goal: A Basic Handbook of Buddhist Meditation,* 77–78. 105. From "The Path of Meditation," in *Karma,* 31–32. 106. From "Sudden Glimpse," in *Glimpses of Mahayana,* 31–32. 107. From "The King of Basic Goodness," in *Great Eastern Sun: The Wisdom of Shambhala,* 95. 108. From "Why We Are Here at All," in *Glimpses of Realization: The Three Bodies of Enlightenment,* 6. 109. From "The Fourth Moment," in *Shambhala Sun* 14, no. 4 (March 2006), 47. 110. From Talk Twelve of *The Tibetan Buddhist Path.*

111. From "A Golden Buddha," in *Glimpses of Mahayana,* 13. 112. From "Ultimate and Relative Bodhichitta," in *Training the Mind and Cultivating Loving-Kindness,* 12. 113. From "The Question of Magic," in *Journey without Goal: The Tantric Wisdom of the Buddha,* 110–11. 114. From "Choiceless Magic," in *Dharma Art,* 92. 115. From "Maha Ati," in *Journey without Goal: The Tantric Wisdom of the Buddha,* 138–39. 116. From Talk Two of *Meditation: The Way of the Buddha.* 117. From "Blamelessness: How to Love Yourself," in *Great Eastern Sun: The Wisdom of Shambhala,* 122–23. 118. From "Ultimate and Relative Bodhichitta," in *Training the Mind and Cultivating Loving-Kindness,* 11–12. 119. From Talk Five of *Warriorship in the Three Yanas.* 120. From "The Six Realms of Being," in *Transcending Madness: The Experience of the Six Bardos,* 51.

121. From "Dathun Letter." 122. From "The Martial Arts and the Art of War," in *The Collected Works of Chögyam Trungpa,* 8:413. 123. From "Ultimate and Relative Bodhichitta," in *Training the Mind and Cultivating Loving-Kindness,* 13–14. 124. From "The Bardo of Illusory Body," in *Transcending Madness: The Experience of the Six Bardos,* 102. 125. From "The Preparation for Tantra," in *The Lion's Roar: An Introduction to Tantra,* 35–36. 126. From "Ultimate and Relative Bodhichitta," in *Training the Mind and Cultivating Loving-Kindness,* 14–15. 127. From "Blamelessness: How to Love Yourself," in *Great Eastern Sun: The Wisdom of Shambhala,* 120. 128. From "Light-Heartedness," in *Glimpses of Realization: The Three Bodies of Enlightenment,* 45–46. 129. From "The Six Realms of Being," in *Transcending Madness: The Experience of the Six Bardos,* 40–41. 130. From "The Fourth Moment," in *Shambhala Sun* 14, no. 4 (March 2006), 47.

131. From "The Six Realms of Being," in *Transcending Madness: The Experience of the Six Bardos,* 42. 132. From "Dome Darshan," in *The Collected Works of Chögyam Trungpa,* 3:545. 133. From Talk Two of *Medi-*

tation: The Way of the Buddha. 134. From "How to Cultivate the Great Eastern Sun," in *Great Eastern Sun: The Wisdom of Shambhala,* 109–10. 135. From "Theism and Non-theism," in *Speaking of Silence: Christians and Buddhists in Dialogue,* 154. 136. From "Natural Hierarchy," in *Shambhala: The Sacred Path of the Warrior,* 113. 137. From "Point Four and the Paramita of Exertion," in *Training the Mind and Cultivating Loving-Kindness,* 130. 138. From "Sudden Glimpse," in *Glimpses of Mahayana,* 36, 38–39. 139. From "Ultimate and Relative Bodhichitta," in *Training the Mind and Cultivating Loving-Kindness,* 11. 140. From "The Realm of the Gods," in *Transcending Madness: The Experience of the Six Bardos,* 202.

141. From "A Golden Buddha," in *Glimpses of Mahayana,* 11–12. 142. From "The Wheel of Life," in *The Collected Works of Chögyam Trungpa,* 3:483. 143. From "Authentic Presence," in *Shambhala: The Sacred Path of the Warrior,* Shambhala Library ed., 198. 144. From "The Question of Magic," in *Journey without Goal: The Tantric Wisdom of the Buddha,* 113–14. 145. From "The Way of the Bodhisattva," in *The Collected Works of Chögyam Trungpa,* 1:452–53. 146. From "Disciplines of Mind Training," in *Training the Mind and Cultivating Loving-Kindness,* Shambhala Library ed., 1, 147. 147. From "Synchronizing Mind and Body," in *Shambhala: The Sacred Path of the Warrior,* Shambhala Library ed., 42–43. 148. From "The Basic Body," in *The Lion's Roar: An Introduction to Tantra,* 46. 149. From "Fantasy and Reality," in *The Myth of Freedom and the Way of Meditation,* Shambhala Library ed., 6–7. 150. From "Suffering, Impermanence, Egolessness," in *The Lion's Roar: An Introduction to Tantra,* 80.

151. From "The Razor's Edge," in *Orderly Chaos: The Mandala Principle,* 18–19. 152. From "Competing with Our Projections," in *The Lion's Roar: An Introduction to Tantra,* 90, 98. 153. From Talk Three of *Meditation: The Way of the Buddha.* 154. From "Trungmase and the

Three Idiots," in *Mishap Lineage: The Line of the Trungpas.* 155. From "Pragmatism and Practice: An Interview with Chögyam Trungpa," in *The Collected Works of Chögyam Trungpa,* 8:432. 156. From "One Stroke" in *Dharma Art,* 98–99. 157. From "The Bardo of Birth," in *Transcending Madness: The Experience of the Six Bardos,* 89–90. 158. From "Buddha Is Everywhere," in *Glimpses of Realization: The Three Bodies of Enlightenment,* 73. 159. From "Blamelessness: How to Love Yourself," in *Great Eastern Sun: The Wisdom of Shambhala,* 122–23. 160. From "Synchronizing Mind and Body," in *Shambhala: The Sacred Path of the Warrior,* Shambhala Library ed., 42–43.

161. From "Recollecting the Present," in *The Path Is the Goal: A Basic Handbook of Buddhist Meditation,* 72–73. 162. From "The Four Foundations of Mindfulness," in *The Heart of the Buddha,* 31. 163. From "Attaining the Higher Realms," in *Great Eastern Sun: The Wisdom of Shambhala,* 133. 164. From "How to Rule," in *Shambhala: The Sacred Path of the Warrior,* 115. 165. From "The Life and Example of Buddha," in *Meditation in Action,* Shambhala Library ed., 16–17. 166. From Talk One of *Meditation: The Way of the Buddha.* 167. From "The Bodhisattva Vow," in *1979 Hinayana-Mahayana Seminary,* 80. 168. From "Just the Facts," in *Elephant,* Summer 2007, 32. 169. From "The Origins of Suffering," in *1975 Hinayana-Mahayana Seminary,* 57. 170. From "Egolessness," in *The Myth of Freedom and the Way of Meditation,* Shambhala Library ed., 21.

171. From "Entering Mahayana: Sugatagharba" in *1982 Hinayana-Mahayana Seminary,* 71. 172. From "Sacredness: Natural Law and Order," in *Great Eastern Sun: The Wisdom of Shambhala,* 90. 173. From "Just the Facts," in *Elephant,* Summer 2007, 32. 174. From "Simplicity," in *The Myth of Freedom and the Way of Meditation,* 44–45. 175. From "A Sense of Humor," in *Cutting Through Spiritual Materialism,* 114–15. 176.

From "Just the Facts," in *Elephant,* Summer 2007, 32. 177. From *Shambhala: The Sacred Path of the Warrior Book and Card Set.* 178. From "The True Spiritual Path," in *The Essential Chögyam Trungpa,* 46. 179. From "Challenge from a Wise Demoness," in *Songs of Milarepa.* 180. From "The True Spiritual Path," in *The Essential Chögyam Trungpa,* 46.

181. From "The Tantric Journey," in *Journey without Goal: The Tantric Wisdom of the Buddha,* 122–23. 182. From "Trungmase and the Three Idiots," in *Mishap Lineage: The Line of the Trungpas.* 183. From "Trungmase and the Three Idiots," *Mishap Lineage: The Line of the Trungpas.* 184. From "The King of Basic Goodness," in *Great Eastern Sun: The Wisdom of Shambhala,* 94. 185. From "How to Rule," in *Shambhala: The Sacred Path of the Warrior,* 116–17. 186. From "Heaven, Earth and Man," in *Dharma Art,* 111. 187. From "Ratna Society Meeting." 188. From "The True Spiritual Path," in *The Essential Chögyam Trungpa,* 46–47. 189. From "Choiceless Magic," in *Dharma Art,* 91–92. 190. From "Nontheistic Energy," in *Journey without Goal: The Tantric Wisdom of the Buddha,* 39, 40, 45.

191. From "Heaven, Earth and Man," in *Dharma Art,* 112–13. 192. From "Humbleness Is the Dwelling Place of the Forefathers," in *1981 Hinayana-Mahayana Seminary,* 39. 193. From "Discipline in the Four Seasons," in *Great Eastern Sun: The Wisdom of Shambhala,* 63. 194. From "Helping Others," in *Great Eastern Sun: The Wisdom of Shambhala,* 176. 195. From "Freedom from Illbirth," in *1974 Hinayana-Mahayana Seminary,* 46. 196. From *Shambhala: The Sacred Path of the Warrior Book and Card Set.* 197. From "Conquering Fear" in *The Collected Works of Chögyam Trungpa,* 8:394–95. 198. From "Discovering Magic," in *Shambhala: The Sacred Path of the Warrior,* Shambhala Dragon ed., 99–100. 199. From "Foreword" to *The Superhuman Life of Gesar of Ling,* in *The Collected Works of Chögyam Trungpa,* 8:411. 200.

From "How to Invoke Magic," in *Shambhala: The Sacred Path of the Warrior,* 108–9.

201. From "Auspicious Coincidence," in *Glimpses of Abhidharma,* Shambhala Dragon ed., 99–100. 202. From "Awareness and Suffering" in *1974 Hinayana-Mahayana Seminary,* 78. 203. From "Auspicious Coincidence," in *Glimpses of Abhidharma,* Shambhala Dragon ed., 99–100. 204. From "Foreword" to *The Superhuman Life of Gesar of Ling,* in *The Collected Works of Chögyam Trungpa,* 8:411. 205. From "The Meeting of Buddhist and Western Psychology," in *The Sanity We Are Born With: A Buddhist Approach to Psychology,* 8–9. 206. From "The Way of the Buddha," in *The Myth of Freedom and the Way of Meditation,* Shambhala Classic ed., 58–59. 207. From "The Meeting of Buddhist and Western Psychology," in *The Sanity We Are Born With: A Buddhist Approach to Psychology,* 9–10. 208. From "Exertion," in *1982 Hinayana-Mahayana Seminary,* 113–14. 209. From "Dome Darshan," in *The Collected Works of Chögyam Trungpa,* 3:539, 545–46. 210. From "The Martial Arts and the Art of War," in *The Collected Works of Chögyam Trungpa,* 8:413–14.

211. From *Shambhala: The Sacred Path of the Warrior Book and Card Set.* 212. From "The Meeting of Buddhist and Western Psychology," in *The Sanity We Are Born With: A Buddhist Approach to Psychology,* 9. 213. From "How to Invoke Magic," in *Shambhala: The Sacred Path of the Warrior,* Shambhala Dragon ed., 107. 214. From "The Meeting of Buddhist and Western Psychology," in *The Sanity We Are Born With: A Buddhist Approach to Psychology,* 10. 215. From "Meditation," in *Dharma Art,* 20. 216. From "Conquering Fear," in *The Collected Works of Chögyam Trungpa,* 8:406. 217. From "Exertion," in *1983 Hinayana-Mahayana Seminary,* 112–13. 218. From "Authentic Presence," in *Shambhala: The Sacred Path of the Warrior,* Shambhala Dragon ed., 168–69. 219. From

"Creating an Environment of Sanity," in *The Sanity We Are Born With: A Buddhist Approach to Psychology,* 145. 220. From "Creating an Environment of Sanity," in *The Sanity We Are Born With: A Buddhist Approach to Psychology,* 148–49.

221. From "The Big No," in *Great Eastern Sun: The Wisdom of Shambhala,* 141. 222. From "Exertion," in *1982 Hinayana-Mahayana Seminary,* 116. 223. From "Intrinsic Health," in *The Sanity We Are Born With: A Buddhist Approach to Psychology,* 163–64. 224. From "Foreword" to *The Superhuman Life of Gesar of Ling,* in *The Collected Works of Chögyam Trungpa,* 8:408. 225. From "Ultimate and Relative Bodhichitta," in *Training the Mind and Cultivating Loving-Kindness,* 1993 ed., 16–17. 226. From "Exertion," in *1982 Hinayana-Mahayana Seminary,* 114–16. 227. From "Exertion," in *1982 Hinayana-Mahayana Seminary,* 119–20. 228. From "The Fourth Moment," in *Shambhala Sun* 14, no. 4 (March 2006), 43. 229. From "The Tantric Journey," in *Journey without Goal: The Tantric Wisdom of the Buddha,* 120. 230. From "Dome Darshan" in *The Collected Works of Chögyam Trungpa,* 3:546.

231. From "Introduction," in *Cutting Through Spiritual Materialism,* Shambhala Dragon ed., 8–9. 232. From "Maha Ati," in *Journey without Goal: The Tantric Wisdom of the Buddha,* 141. 233. From "Introduction," in *Cutting Through Spiritual Materialism,* Shambhala Dragon ed., 9–10. 234. From "Authentic Presence," in *Shambhala: The Sacred Path of the Warrior,* Shambhala Dragon ed., 164. 235. From "Is Meditation Therapy?" in *The Sanity We Are Born With: A Buddhist Approach to Psychology,* 184–86. 236. From "The Four Foundations of Mindfulness," in *The Heart of the Buddha,* 46. 237. From "Humbleness Is the Dwelling Place of the Forefathers," in *1981 Hinayana-Mahayana Seminary,* 39–40. 238. From "Discovering Bodhicitta," in *1981 Hinayana-Mahayana Seminary,* 87. 239. From "Cosmic Disaster," in *Glimpses of*

Realization: The Three Bodies of Enlightenment, 14. 240. From "Foreword" to *The Superhuman Life of Gesar of Ling*, in *The Collected Works of Chögyam Trungpa*, 8:411.

241. From "The Meeting of Buddhist and Western Psychology," in *The Sanity We Are Born With: A Buddhist Approach to Psychology*, 7. 242. From "Money." 243. From "The Way of the Buddha" in *The Myth of Freedom and the Way of Meditation*, 57–58. 244. From "Vipashyana Awareness," in *1981 Hinayana-Mahayana Seminary*, 33. 245. From *Shambhala: The Sacred Path of the Warrior Book and Card Set*. 246. From "The Ultimate Truth Is Fearless." 247. From "Renunciation and Daring," in *Shambhala: The Sacred Path of the Warrior*, Shambhala Library ed., 63–64. 248. From "The Meeting of Buddhist and Western Psychology," in *The Sanity We Are Born With: A Buddhist Approach to Psychology*, 7. 249. From "The Ultimate Truth Is Fearless." 250. From "Peace."

251. From "The Ultimate Truth Is Fearless." 252. From "Foreword" to *The Superhuman Life of Gesar of Ling*, in *The Collected Works of Chögyam Trungpa*, 8:411–12. 253. From "Me-ness and the Emotions," in *The Path Is the Goal: A Basic Handbook of Buddhist Meditation*, 59–60. 254. From "Exertion," in *1982 Hinayana-Mahayana Seminary*, 120–21. 255. From *Collected Vajra Assemblies*, 1:240–41. 256. From *The Warrior's Way*, 11. 257. From "Foreword" to *The Superhuman Life of Gesar of Ling*, in *The Collected Works of Chögyam Trungpa*, 8:409. 258. From "The Bodhisattva Vow," in *1979 Hinayana-Mahayana Seminary*, 80. 259. From "The Way of the Buddha," in *The Myth of Freedom and the Way of Meditation*, 58. 260. From "The Fourth Moment," in *Shambhala Sun* 14, no. 4 (March 2006), 44–45.

261. From "Authentic Presence," in *Shambhala: The Sacred Path of the Warrior*, Shambhala Dragon ed., 165–66, 167. 262. From *The Warrior's*

Way, 14–15. 263. From "The Bodhisattva Vow," in *The Heart of the Buddha,* 111. 264. From "The Shambhala Lineage," in *Shambhala: The Sacred Path of the Warrior,* Shambhala Library ed., 211. 265. From "The Bodhisattva Vow" in *The Heart of the Buddha,* 108–9. 266. From "The Bodhisattva Vow" in *The Heart of the Buddha,* 111–13. 267. From "Conquering Fear" in *The Collected Works of Chögyam Trungpa,* 8:395–96. 268. From "Authentic Presence," in *Shambhala: The Sacred Path of the Warrior,* Shambhala Dragon ed., 167–68. 269. From "Point Three: Transformation of Bad Circumstances" in *Training the Mind and Cultivating Loving-Kindness,* 1993 ed., 88–89. 270. From "The Bodhisattva Vow," in *The Heart of the Buddha,* 113.

271. From "Explanation of the Vajra Guru Mantra" in *The Collected Works of Chögyam Trungpa,* 5:323. 272. From "The Mishap Lineage," in *Mishap Lineage: The Line of the Trungpas.* 273. From "Self-Existing Grin," in *Glimpses of Realization: The Three Bodies of Enlightenment,* 33–34. 274. From "Conquering Fear," in *The Collected Works of Chögyam Trungpa,* 8:400–401. 275. From Talk Nine of *The Tibetan Buddhist Path.* 276. From "The Achievement of Enlightenment" in *1974 Hinayana-Mahayana Seminary,* 164. 277. From "Let the Phenomena Play," in *Crazy Wisdom,* 57–58. 278. From "Sacred World," in *Shambhala: The Sacred Path of the Warrior,* Shambhala Library ed., 141. 279. From "Awakening Buddha Nature," in *Glimpses of Mahayana,* 19. 280. From Talk Ten of *The Tibetan Buddhist Path.*

281. From "Heaven, Earth and Man," in *Dharma Art,* 113–14. 282. From "What Is the Heart of the Buddha?" in *The Heart of the Buddha,* 6. 283. From "Awakening Buddha Nature," in *Glimpses of Mahayana,* 21–22. 284. From Talk Five of *Warriorship in the Three Yanas.* 285. From "The Mahasattva Avalokiteshvara," in *The Collected Works of Chögyam Trungpa,* 1:450–51. 286. From "Nowness," in *Shambhala: The Sacred Path

of the Warrior, 91. 287. From "The Four Foundations of Mindfulness," in *The Heart of the Buddha*, 44. 288. From "Conquering Fear," in *The Collected Works of Chögyam Trungpa*, 8:397. 289. From "Awaken ing Buddha Nature," in *Glimpses of Mahayana*, 19. 290. From Talk Nine of *The Tibetan Buddhist Path*.

291. From "Form," in *Glimpses of Abhidharma*, 12. 292. From "Auspicious Coincidence," in *Glimpses of Abhidharma*, 95. 293. From "From Raw Eggs to Stepping-Stones" in *The Path Is the Goal: A Basic Handbook of Buddhist Meditation*, 116. 294. From "Consciousness," in *Glimpses of Abhidharma*, 80–81. 295. From "The Four Foundations of Mindfulness," in *The Heart of the Buddha*, 33. 296. From "The Martial Arts and the Art of War," in *The Collected Works of Chögyam Trungpa*, 8: 414–16. 297. From "The Four Foundations of Mindfulness," in *The Heart of the Buddha*, 33–34. 298. From "Fantasy and Reality," in *The Myth of Freedom and the Way of Meditation*, Shambhala Library ed., 6–7. 299. From "Genuine Madness and Pop Art" in *Illusion's Game: The Life and Teaching of Naropa*, 30–31. 300. From "The Four Foundations of Mindfulness," in *The Heart of the Buddha*, 36.

301. From Talk One of *Warriorship in the Three Yanas*. 302. From "Basic Goodness, a Talk to Directors of Shambhala Training." 303. From *Shambhala: The Sacred Path of the Warrior Book and Card Set*. 304. From "The Lion's Roar," in *Crazy Wisdom*, 142–43. 305. From Talk One of *Warriorship in the Three Yanas*. 306. From Talk One of *Warriorship in the Three Yanas*. 307. From "Very Practical Joke" in *The Teacup and the Skullcup: Chögyam Trungpa on Zen and Tantra*, 4–7. 308. From "The Four Foundations of Mindfulness," in *The Heart of the Buddha*, 36. 309. From "Very Practical Joke" in *The Teacup and the Skullcup: Chögyam Trungpa on Zen and Tantra*, 4–5. 310. From *Shambhala: The Sacred Path of the Warrior Book and Card Set*.

311. From "The Four Foundations of Mindfulness," in *The Heart of the Buddha,* 32–33. 312. From "Artists and Unemployed Samurai," in *The Teacup and the Skullcup: Chögyam Trungpa on Zen and Tantra,* 42. 313. From "Transpersonal Cooperation at Naropa," in *The Collected Works of Chögyam Trungpa,* 2:628–29. 314. From "The Lion's Roar," in *Crazy Wisdom,* 142. 315. From "The Razor's Edge," in *Orderly Chaos: The Mandala Principle,* 16–17. 316. From "Back to Square One," in *Dharma Art,* 119, 120, 122, 123. 317. From "Meditation," in *Meditation in Action,* Shambhala Library ed., 85. 318. From "The Kingdom, the Cocoon, the Great Eastern Sun," in *Great Eastern Sun: The Wisdom of Shambhala,* 7. 319. From "Consciousness," in *Glimpses of Abhidharma,* 80. 320. From "The Four Foundations of Mindfulness," in *The Heart of the Buddha,* 33–35.

321. From "Dynamic Stillness and Cosmic Absorption," in *The Teacup and the Skullcup: Chögyam Trungpa on Zen and Tantra,* 99. 322. From "Auspicious Coincidence," in *Glimpses of Abhidharma,* 101–2. 323. From "Aggression," in *The Four Dharmas of Gampopa,* 16–17. 324. From "Consciousness," in *Glimpses of Abhidharma,* 74–75. 325. From "Back to Square One," in *Dharma Art,* 126–27. 326. From "Consciousness," in *Glimpses of Abhidharma,* 78–79. 327. From *Shambhala: The Sacred Path of the Warrior Book and Card Set.* 328. From "Endless Richness," in *Dharma Art,* 116–17. 329. From "Natural Hierarchy," in *The Collected Works of Chögyam Trungpa,* 8:435. 330. From "Natural Hierarchy," in *The Collected Works of Chögyam Trungpa,* 8:435–36.

331. From "Conquering Fear," in *The Collected Works of Chögyam Trungpa,* 8:403. 332. From "The Martial Arts and the Art of War," in *The Collected Works of Chögyam Trungpa,* 8:415. 333. From "Auspicious Coincidence," in *Glimpses of Abhidharma,* 101. 334. From "From Raw Eggs to Stepping-Stones," in *The Path Is the Goal: A Basic Handbook of*

Buddhist Meditation, 118. 335. From "Creating an Environment of Sanity," in *The Sanity We Are Born With: A Buddhist Approach to Psychology,* 145–46. 336. From "Maha Ati," in *Journey without Goal: The Tantric Wisdom of the Buddha,* 133–34. 337. From Talk Two of *Warriorship in the Three Yanas.* 338. From "The Way of the Buddha," in *The Myth of Freedom and the Way of Meditation,* 56–57. 339. From "Practice and Basic Goodness: A Talk to Children," in *The Heart of the Buddha,* 193–94. 340. From "Save Yourself," in *Elephant,* Spring 2007, 30.

341. From "The Birth of Karma," in *Karma,* 5. 342. From "Patience," in *Meditation in Action,* Shambhala Pocket Classic ed., 85. 343. From "Past, Present, and Future," in *Karma,* 13–14. 344. From "The Four Foundations of Mindfulness," in *The Heart of the Buddha,* 35. 345. From "A Question of Heart," in *Great Eastern Sun: The Wisdom of Shambhala,* 191–92. 346. From Talk One of *Work, Sex, and Money.* 347. From "A Question of Heart," in *Great Eastern Sun: The Wisdom of Shambhala,* 192. 348. From "Generosity," in *Meditation in Action,* Shambhala Library ed., 52–54. 349. From "The Birth of Ego," in *The Sanity We Are Born With: A Buddhist Approach to Psychology,* 79–80. 350. From "From Raw Eggs to Stepping-Stones," in *The Path Is the Goal: A Basic Handbook of Buddhist Meditation,* 119.

351. From "The Cosmic Sneeze," in *Great Eastern Sun: The Wisdom of Shambhala,* 58–59. 352. From "Mirrorlike Wisdom," in *Great Eastern Sun: The Wisdom of Shambhala,* 75. 353. From "Generosity," in *Meditation in Action,* Shambhala Library ed., 60–61. 354. From *Shambhala: The Sacred Path of the Warrior Book and Card Set.* 355. From "Becoming a Full Human Being," in *The Sanity We Are Born With: A Buddhist Approach to Psychology,* 139. 356. From "Becoming a Full Human Being," in *The Sanity We Are Born With: A Buddhist Approach to Psychology,* 141. 357. From "Generosity," in *Meditation in Action,* Shambhala Library ed., 63. 358. From

"Past, Present, and Future," in *Karma,* 16. 359. From "Becoming a Full Human Being," in *The Sanity We Are Born With: A Buddhist Approach to Psychology,* 142. 360. From "Creating an Environment of Sanity," in *The Sanity We Are Born With: A Buddhist Approach to Psychology,* 147.

361. From "Wise Fool," in *Dharma Art,* 75. 362. From "Maha Ati," in *Journey without Goal: The Tantric Wisdom of the Buddha,* 137. 363. From "Conquering Fear," in *The Collected Works of Chögyam Trungpa,* 8:397. 364. From "Helping Others," in *Great Eastern Sun: The Wisdom of Shambhala,* 175–76. 365. From "Maha Ati," in *Journey without Goal: The Tantric Wisdom of the Buddha,* 142.

BIBLIOGRAPHY

Books

The Collected Works of Chögyam Trungpa. Edited by Carolyn Rose Gimian. 8 vols. Boston: Shambhala, 2003 and 2004.

Crazy Wisdom. Edited by Sherab Chödzin. Boston: Shambhala, 1991.

Cutting Through Spiritual Materialism. Edited by John Baker and Marvin Casper. Boston: Shambhala, 1973; Shambhala Classic ed., 2002; Shambhala Dragon ed., 1987.

Dharma Art. Edited by Judith L. Lief. Boston: Shambhala, 1996.

The Essential Chögyam Trungpa. Edited by Carolyn Rose Gimian. Boston: Shambhala, 2000.

Glimpses of Abhidharma: From a Seminar on Buddhist Psychology. Boulder: Prajna, 1978; Shambhala Dragon ed., 1987.

Glimpses of Mahayana. Edited by Judith L. Lief. Halifax: Vajradhatu, 2001.

Glimpses of Realization: The Three Bodies of Enlightenment. Edited by Judith L. Lief. Halifax: Vajradhatu, 2006.

Glimpses of Space: The Feminine Principle and Evam. Edited by Judith L. Lief. Halifax: Vajradhatu, 1999.

Great Eastern Sun: The Wisdom of Shambhala. Edited by Carolyn Rose Gimian. Boston: Shambhala, 1999.

The Heart of the Buddha. Edited by Judith L. Lief. Boston: Shambhala, 1991.

Illusion's Game: The Life and Teaching of Naropa. Edited by Sherab Chödzin. Boston: Shambhala, 1994.

Journey without Goal: The Tantric Wisdom of the Buddha. Edited by Carolyn Rose Gimian. Boston: Shambhala, 1981.

Lion's Roar: An Introduction to Tantra. Edited by Sherab Chödzin. Boston: Shambhala, 1992.

Meditation in Action. Edited by Richard Arthure. Boston: Shambhala, 1969; Shamhala Pocket Clasic ed., 1996; Shambhala Library ed., 2004.

Mishap Lineage: The Line of the Trungpas. Edited by Carolyn Rose Gimian. Halifax: Vajradhatu, forthcoming.

The Myth of Freedom and the Way of Meditation. Edited by John Baker and Marvin Casper. Boston: Shambhala, 1976; Shambhala Classic ed., 2002; Shambhala Dragon ed., 1988; Shambhala Library ed., 2005.

Orderly Chaos: The Mandala Principle. Edited by Sherab Chödzin. Boston: Shambhala, 1991.

The Path Is the Goal: A Basic Handbook of Buddhist Meditation. Edited by Sherab Chödzin. Boston: Shambhala, 1995.

The Sanity We Are Born With: A Buddhist Approach to Psychology. Edited by Carolyn Rose Gimian. Boston: Shambhala, 2005.

Shambhala: The Sacred Path of the Warrior. Edited by Carolyn Rose Gimian. Boston: Shambhala, 1984; Shambhala Dragon ed., 1988; Shambhala Library ed., 2003.

The Teacup and the Skullcup: Chögyam Trungpa on Zen and Tantra. Edited by Judith L. Lief and David Schneider. Halifax: Vajradhatu, 2007.

Training the Mind and Cultivating Loving-Kindness. Edited by Judith L. Lief. Boston: Shambhala, 1993; Shambhala Library ed., 2005.

Transcending Madness: The Experience of the Six Bardos. Edited by Judith L. Lief. Boston: Shambhala, 1992.

Other Sources

"Basic Goodness, a Talk to Directors of Shambhala Training." Unpublished transcript, January 1978.

Collected Vajra Assemblies. Vol. 1. Halifax: Vajradhatu, 1990.
"Dathun Letter." Unpublished transcript, circa 1973.
"Disappointment." *Tibet Journal* 2, no. 4 (Winter 1977): 37–40.
The Four Dharmas of Gampopa. Sourcebook. Halifax: Vajradhatu, 1975.
"The Fourth Moment." *Shambhala Sun* 14, no. 4 (March 2006), 42–48, 92–95.
"Just the Facts." *Elephant,* Summer 2007, 32.
Karma. Sourcebook. Halifax: Vajradhatu, 1975.
Meditation: The Way of the Buddha. Unpublished transcript of a five-talk seminar, Naropa Institute, Boulder, Colo., June 1974.
"Money." Unpublished transcript of a talk, Scotland, ca. March 29, 1969.
"A New Year's Message." Unpublished transcript of a talk delivered for the Tibetan New Year, 1981.
1974 *Hinayana-Mahayana Seminary.* Sourcebook. Halifax: Vajradhatu, 1975.
1975 *Hinayana-Mahayana Seminary.* Sourcebook. Halifax: Vajradhatu, 1976.
1979 *Hinayana-Mahayana Seminary.* Sourcebook. Halifax: Vajrad-hatu, 1980.
1981 *Hinayana-Mahayana Seminary.* Sourcebook. Halifax: Vajradhatu, 1982.
1982 *Hinayana-Mahayana Seminary.* Sourcebook. Halifax: Vajradhatu, 1983.
1983 *Hinayana-Mahayana Seminary.* Sourcebook. Halifax: Vajradhatu, 1984.
"Peace." Unpublished transcript of a talk, Scotland, ca. March 29, 1969.
"The Positive Aspect of Suffering." Unpublished transcript of a talk, Scotland, ca. 1969.
"Ratna Society Meeting." Unpublished transcript, August 28, 1978.
"Remarks at the Opening Ceremony of Samye Ling Meditation Centre in Scotland." Unpublished transcript, ca. 1967.
"Save Yourself." *Elephant,* Spring 2007, 30.

Selected Community Talks. Sourcebook. Halifax: Vajradhatu, 1978.
Shambhala: The Sacred Path of the Warrior Book and Card Set—53 Principles for Living Life with Fearlessness and Gentleness. Boston: Shambhala, 2004.
Songs of Milarepa. Unpublished transcript of a sixteen-talk seminar, Barnet, Vt., Summer 1970.
"Theism and Non-Theism." In *Speaking of Silence: Christians and Buddhists in Dialogue,* compiled and edited by Susan Walker, 154. Halifax: Vajradhatu, 2005.
The Tibetan Buddhist Path. Unpublished transcript of a thirteen-talk seminar, Naropa Institute, Boulder, Colo., July 1974.
"The Ultimate Truth Is Fearless." Unpublished transcript of a talk. Boulder, Colorado, February 25, 1972.
The Warrior's Way. Sourcebook. Halifax: Vajradhatu, 1983.
Warriorship in the Three Yanas. Unpublished transcript of a five-talk seminar, Rocky Mountain Dharma Center, August 1978.
Work, Sex, and Money. Unpublished transcript of a three-talk seminar, Burlington, Vt., April 1972.

FURTHER READINGS AND RESOURCES

Books

The Sanity We Are Born With: A Buddhist Approach to Psychology is an excellent overview of Chögyam Trungpa's writings on the Buddhist view of mind, the practice of meditation, and the application of the Buddhist teachings to working with oneself and others in the field of psychology. Additional discussion of the practice of meditation overall and an in-depth treatment of mindfulness and awareness (*shamatha* and *vipashyana*) meditation is provided by Chögyam Trungpa in *The Path Is the Goal: A Basic Handbook of Buddhist Meditation.* The discussion of awareness practice is particularly well developed in this small manual on Buddhist practice.

Cultivating loving-kindness and compassion toward all beings is at the root of Chögyam Trungpa's approach to working with others. *Training the Mind and Cultivating Loving-Kindness* presents fifty-nine slogans, or aphorisms related to meditation practice, that show a practical path to making friends with oneself and developing compassion for others.

For readers interested in an overview of the Buddhist path, the following volumes are recommended: *Cutting Through Spiritual Materialism, The Myth of Freedom and the Way of Meditation,* and *The Essential Chögyam Trungpa.*

The Shambhala path of warriorship offers heartfelt advice on transforming fear and anxiety into gentle bravery, so that one develops confidence and skill in working with others. These teachings on basic goodness and how to be more self-assured, yet genuine and vulnerable, in one's life are available in *Shambhala: The Sacred Path of the Warrior* and *Great Eastern Sun: The Wisdom of Shambhala. Shambhala: The Sacred Path of the Warrior Book and Card Set* provides a small handbook and a group of slogan cards that can be used to contemplate these teachings on working with oneself and others.

Other Resources

Ocean of Dharma Quotes of the Week brings you the teachings of Chögyam Trungpa Rinpoche. An e-mail is sent out several times each week containing a quote from Chögyam Trungpa's extensive teachings. Quotations of material may be from unpublished material, forthcoming publications, or previously published sources. Ocean of Dharma Quotes of the Week are selected by Carolyn Rose Gimian. To enroll, go to www.oceanofdharma.com.

For information regarding meditation instruction, please visit the Web site of Shambhala International at www.shambhala.org. This Web site contains information about the more than one hundred centers affiliated with Shambhala.

The Chögyam Trungpa Legacy Project is an independent nonprofit foundation being incorporated in the United States, in Canada (as a charitable organization) and eventually in Europe. It was established to help preserve, disseminate, and expand Chögyam Trungpa's legacy. The Legacy Project supports the preservation, propagation, and publication of Trungpa Rinpoche's dharma teachings. This includes plans for the creation of a comprehensive virtual archive and learning community. For information, go to http://ChogyamTrungpa.com

For publications from Vajradhatu Publications and Kalapa Recordings, including both books and audiovisual materials, go to www.shambhalashop.com.

For information about the archive of the author's work, please contact the Shambhala Archives: archives@shambhala.org.

ABOUT CHÖGYAM TRUNGPA

Born in Tibet in 1939, Chögyam Trungpa was recognized in infancy as an important reincarnate teacher, or rinpoche. His was the last generation to receive the complete education in the teachings of Buddhism while in Tibet. The abbot of the Surmang Monasteries and the governor of the Surmang District of Eastern Tibet, Trungpa Rinpoche was forced to flee his homeland in 1959 to escape persecution by the communist Chinese. His harrowing journey over the Himalayas to freedom lasted ten months.

After several years in India, where he was the spiritual adviser to the Young Lamas School, Trungpa Rinpoche immigrated to England where he studied at Oxford University and established the Samye Ling Meditation Centre in Scotland. Following a serious auto accident in 1969, which he regarded as a message to be more open and courageous, Trungpa Rinpoche gave up his monastic robes and became a lay teacher, in order to communicate more directly with Western students. In January 1970, he married Diana Judith Pybus and shortly thereafter immigrated to North America, where he remained until his death in Halifax, Nova Scotia, in 1987.

One of the first Tibetan lineage holders to present the Buddhist teachings in English, Chögyam Trungpa's command of the English language and his understanding of the Western mind made him one of the most important influences on the development of Buddhism in the West. He established hundreds of meditation centers throughout North America, founded Naropa University in Boulder, Colorado—the first Buddhist-inspired university in North America—and attracted several thousand committed students, who received advanced teachings from him and have continued to propagate his teachings and lineage in North America. Chögyam Trungpa was also instrumental in bringing many other great Tibetan lineage holders to teach in North America. In 1977, he established Shambhala Training, a program to present meditation and the Shambhala tradition of warriorship to a broad audience. The author of more than two dozen popular books on Buddhism, meditation, and the path of Shambhala warriorship, he was an ecumenical teacher who sought out the wisdom in other schools of Buddhism and in other religions. He also studied and promoted a contemplative awareness of the visual arts, design, poetry, theater, and other aspects of Western art and culture.